The Power

The Power of Ch'i

An Introduction to Chinese Mysticism
and Philosophy

by

Michael Page

THE AQUARIAN PRESS

First published 1988

Excerpts from *Tao and Longevity* by Wen Kuan Chu are used by permission of the publishers, Samuel Weiser Inc., York Beach, Maine 03910, USA.

Excerpt from *Creative Visualisation* by Shakti Gawain © 1978 by Shakti Gawain is reprinted by permission of Whatever Publishing Inc., San Rafael, California, USA.

Quotes from *Confucius: The Analects* translated by D. C. Lau (Penguin Classics, 1979) and reproduced by permission of Penguin Books Ltd, Middx, England.

British Library Cataloguing in Publication Data

Page, Michael
The power of ch'i.
1. Taoist philosophy ch'i — Critical
studies.
I. Title
181'.09514

ISBN 0-85030-764-3

The Aquarian Press is part of the Thorsons Publishing Group, Wellingborough, Northamptonshire, NN8 2RQ, England.

Printed and Bound in Great Britain by
Hartnolls Limited, Bodmin, Cornwall.

3 5 7 9 10 8 6 4

Contents

Preface

This book is about the control of the forces of nature within and without man's own frame. It tells the story of a kind of science.

Western scientists seek to control natural forces, yet they have largely ignored this story that comes from the East. They have thought of it as a story of magic and so not worth considering.

People who live for more than 250 years; martial arts opponents propelled yards with no obvious effort; a change of furniture bringing good fortune; railway companies forced to change plans; miracle cures; addictions mastered; river levels lowered. All these phenomena are believed to have happened. All occur through the harnessing of cosmic energy by Chinese Taoists.

But is it magic or a kind of science?

Sexual alchemy, martial arts, control of the forces of the earth, acupuncture: all these would once have been classed as magic or charlatanism. Now we in the West are not so sure.

One thing all these marvels have in common is that they involve a knowledge of the mysterious power called, in Chinese, ch'i, a word which denotes a vital breath or energy which animates the cosmos.

Does it exist?

The Chinese physical universe is said to consist of an environment of energy which envelops and permeates us. From the smallest cell to the mightiest galaxies in space, from atomic particles to human history, all existence is generated and perpetuated by ch'i.

If there is a universal field of energy that is itself the universe, and if that field maintains the stars in their courses, gives life to the ant, causes Black Holes and keeps each single atom spinning, then it is not surprising that men have tried to harness it for their own ends. That there is such a field is becoming common ground between Taoist mystics and hard headed Western scientists. As Fritjof Capra says in his book, *The Tao of Physics*, 'As in quantum theory, the field—or the ch'i—is not only the underlying essence of all material objects, but also carries their mutual interactions...'

Many westerners say that ch'i has no equivalent in our terminology, that it is unscientific and not provable.

But these opinions are becoming less certain.

It is modern theoretical physics that has altered the thinking. If we look beyond the everyday to realms that are too minute even for electron microscopes, to the world of quantum physics, then we begin to see that we are getting close to the thinking that has been current in the east for thousands of years.

In his book, Capra goes on to say that ch'i is indeed identical to the newly discovered quantum field. 'The Neo-Confucians developed a notion of ch'i which bears the most striking resemblance to the concept of the quantum field in modern physics'. He points to the remarkable similarity of description between ch'i and the quantum field as each being 'a tenuous and non-perceptible form of matter'.

In other words, modern physicists and ancient Chinese unite in saying that each of us exists in ch'i, and ch'i is within us. 'The quantum field, waving and vibrating, rhythmically alternating like the yin and yang, forms things and dissolves them.'

The concept has been current in Chinese thinking since at least the time of Lao Tzu, hundreds of years BC, and has led to investigation and application in the fields of health, ageing, psychological autonomy, magic, geomancy, self-defence, art, and so forth.

But much of what is going wrong in the world nowadays can be laid at the door of western-style science. Such scientists say that all they are trying to do is to control nature for the good of us all.

Is not ch'i another gateway to more effective control? Are there not dangers here?

The difference between western science and eastern is that the west is aggressive, too often going against the grain of nature, whereas people who study ch'i go with the flow: indeed, to do anything else is ultimately not possible. The yin and the yang will maintain harmony, even at the cost of Western hubris.

The study of ch'i reveals that it is possible and advantageous to learn to control the energy: in that way we shall be healthier both physically and mentally, and will create our own good fortune without harm to the environment.

The book, then, starts in the opening two chapters with an explanation and expansion of the basic concept of ch'i and a consideration of the whole concept of change as seen by Taoists. That done, the rest of the book is devoted to an examination of the various fields of knowledge in which ch'i has played a central part.

It is perhaps significant that the concept of ch'i has not before been isolated for examination in this way. This is almost certainly because it is so fundamental to all fields as to be taken for granted. This will have been the case with the Chinese themselves. But for Westerners coming relatively new to Chinese culture, it will hopefully be enlightening.

1.

The Nature of Ch'i

Ch'i as a concept resembles a cut diamond: each face reflecting a different light, yet all emanating from a central unity.

At its least complicated, and that is complicated enough, the central unity represents the cosmic life force in all its variety, the ultimate essence of the universe, enveloping it and moving it from within, permeating all entities of which the cosmos is composed, a part of each and sustaining each. It is at one and the same time the ultimate cause and the ultimate effect, entirely self-contained.

It is thus a vitally meaningful concept for thoughtful people everywhere and at all times: it is a universal concept, and as such it would be surprising if the general idea had been confined to China.

It was not unknown in early Western thought, for instance in the works of the 'Greek Taoist', Heraclitus, with his theory of eternal flux, and it is now once again appearing in the West as a fundamentally important concept in advanced physics: fundamental, that is, in the deepest sense of the word.

In the East, too, there are a number of similar concepts, such as *shakti* or spirit energy, *kundalini* or serpent power, and the Tibetan spirit heat or spirit power.

But beyond all that, it must be remembered that it is a Chinese word for a uniquely Chinese concept in which man is not a separate, distinct and uniquely powerful aspect of the cosmos, but is in reality an integral part of the total, partaking of the nature of the total: a microcosm in macrocosm.

As such it is an aspect not only of Chinese cosmology but very much also of Chinese everyday life: appearing in considerations of Chinese health practices, art, philosophy, science, magic, martial arts, architecture, town planning, business planning and so forth.

The fact, then, that ch'i is an integral part of so many aspects of Chinese culture is an indication that is a fundamental concept to the Chinese in all walks of life: much more so than any similar concept is to the average man in the street of London, Los Angeles, or perhaps even Lhasa.

The fact that it is a universally meaningful concept does not mean that it is a simple or unitary concept. As an aspect of quantum physics, for instance, it is particularly dense. Similarly, its interpretation by the Chinese in terms of their mythology and general world-view, makes it often nearly as dense to a non-Chinese. A further complication is that it appears in practices as far removed from each other, as we shall see, as medicine and magic, each of which tends to have its own dialect within the common language.

Nevertheless, certain regularities do appear: the interplay of yin and yang, for instance, and the theory of the Five Elements.

Ch'i is the principle of change. As such it is far removed from chaos: it is a fundamental belief of practitioners who study and make use of ch'i that cosmic change is cyclic, that it obeys laws, and that these laws can be understood and utilized.

In ancient Taoist writings, and ch'i was known by the time of the I Ching and the Tao Te Ching, the primitive character representing ch'i meant 'no fire'. In other words, if the fires of lust or desire (the secondary fires) were dampened, then one was filled with ch'i (the ruling fire). When one attained mental quietude, real ch'i was generated. This acquisition of real ch'i by the practice of quietude was the aim constantly put forward in the early days of classical Taoism by Chuang Tzu, reinforcing the ideas of Lao Tzu. It is still to be clearly seen in practice in the work of Taoist artists, and in the 'no-mind' generated in the practitioner of martial arts.

Taoism, particularly early Taoism, is a way of life based on rhythm and flux, on the natural harmony of nature. It tends to the unconventional, and exhibits a freedom-loving detachment from wordly things. Its product is the poet, the artist (often in past times tolerated in the royal court when drunk), the metaphysician, the mystic, all of them light-hearted and given to laughter. Its methods, if such they can be called, are based on sitting, 'breathing through the heels', and pursuing a life-style in which worry, ambition and so forth are kept to a minimum, in which beds may be moved so that the gradual blossoming of a flower can be enjoyed in all its magic.

Such men and women are rare today. The original magic was lost as men became more clever and less wise. For as the ages rolled past the initial simplicity was lost. The complicating process gained momentum, in particular when the Confucianists gained influence.

Later the character representing ch'i was made more compli- cated and came to mean ether, breath, vapour, steam, or matter- energy. It seemed that the definitions and perhaps the nature of ch'i as seen by man were multiplying like the ten thousand things, an occurrence which would certainly not have surprised the Old Gentleman, Lao Tzu. It was a tendency that did not cease, and perhaps it reflected the analytic thinking affected first by the Con- fucianists and later by the neo-Confucianists.

Confucianism was much more concerned with the stable order, the formal, the conventional and the practical administration of worldly affairs. There was a heavy emphasis on conformity in the social and physical aspects of life. Taoism thus appears to have lost still more of its original simplicity, except that there were always hermits who retired to mountain caves, perhaps in self- defence. In any case, it was through them that the traditions of early Taoism were maintained. John Blofeld vividly describes his experience in meeting with such living examples.[1]

But, away from the mountains, a high technology began to emerge in the burgeoning sciences of Feng Shui and acupunc- ture, and it appeared that much material benefit could be gained from a study of the manifestations of ch'i and its consequent con- trol. Ch'i itself was seen by the scholars of the time as being totally material. 'The Great Void cannot but consist of ether; this ether cannot but condense to form all things; and these things cannot but become dispersed so as to form once more the Great Void.[2]

This materialism, with its self-contained principle, was too much for some, and many thinkers felt that the picture of creation as being purely and anarchically substantial, without any divine or pseudo-divine principle behind it, was incorrect. They put for- ward a theory that the materialism of ch'i must have some ulti- mate principle that determined its creative character. This principle they referred to as li . 'When a house is built it is constructed of substantial items: brick, wood, mortar. But there must be a plan whereby these substances are organized into a meaningful whole. The material is ch'i, the plan li.[3] It would appear that the truly anarchic principle of Taoism as a breath that bloweth where it listeth was to be lost in a hierarchic downgrading of ch'i.

For the mass of pragmatic Chinese this was splitting unneces-sary hairs. Of course they knew that ch'i was material: sometimes coarse, sometimes subtle, but for all practical purposes, it was mat-ter and as such the material manifestation of the Great Tao, the nameless and indescribable: 'the non-existence that is the antece-dent of heaven and earth.'[4] For the Chinese man in the street, the broad twofold division of ch'i into the ch'i of heaven and the ch'i of man was sufficient. Ch'i continued to be regarded as primal matter, which could often be quite as coarse as it was subtle. The man in the street maintained a belief in a materialistic universe in terms of a primal quality of existence, ch'i, which condensed and constituted itself into the various particularities of the cosmos, including man himself.

Later still, the character of ch'i gained two meanings: heaven's ch'i which encompassed such entities as air, steam, gas and weather; and man's ch'i which included his aura, breath, acupunc-ture channels and bodily fluids. Of the two, man's ch'i was the weaker: it was strongly influenced by the ch'i from heaven and earth, though it was possible to counter these influences to an extent by the use of art, craft, magic, and science. This was felt to be the case because it was believed that all things, animate and inanimate, large and small, natural and artificial, inhaled and exhaled ch'i and thus affected one another.

Man's ch'i, because heavily influenced by the ch'i of heaven, has always been the main subject of attention: men and women have always looked for happiness and good fortune, and it appeared that attention to the flow of ch'i made these more likely.

Such attention indicates that ch'i does not have a fixed form: agent of change it may be, but it is not itself free from change. So it is seen that there are two chief ways in which bodily ch'i can be manifested. Depending on the various factors in a per-son's life, such as birth date, or the material circumstances of life, ch'i can become weak or strong. Whatever form it takes, ch'i is energy expressed in material form: light, strong and subtle ch'i floats as air; heavy, weak and coarse ch'i sinks to form solid sub-stance.

When it is strong, it manifests itself as thermal energy or fevers, or it may be vaporized as in sweating or moist palms, or it may be ionized as in martial arts. In this subtle form it is a vitality which may in fact be quite indistinguishable (except by temporary location) from its cosmic counterpart, the ch'i of heaven.

In its weak or coarse form, ch'i is not precisely identical to but is closely associated with, and conveyed in, the air breathed in through the lungs, kidneys and pores. It may indeed be entirely visible as a liquid in sweating, diarrhea, and runny noses, as well as in seminal and vaginal discharge.

So it is clear that both subtle and coarse ch'i may be breathed in, and one of the aims of the mystic is to convert the coarse weak ch'i into its subtle strong form, the better to achieve harmony with the Tao. For this, breathing exercises may be used and the object of these was often to animate the subtle ch'i that was already present in the body. Breathing coarse ch'i caused the subtle ch'i to stir.[5]

In order to better unite mind and matter and animate the being, ch'i does not have a fixed form. But, in whatever form it does manifest, it animates all the processes of the body: digestion, assimilation, evacuation; breathing in and out; blood circulation; and the dissemination of fluids throughout the body.

But it does not only animate the lower functions of the body. In addition, it animates the higher functions of the mind: we shall see its functions in the martial arts, and we shall see in painting, for example, how the creative ch'i flows through the body, the arm, the brush and then on to silk or paper, 'thus uniting artist with creation'.

As can be seen in the martial arts, every movement of ch'i influences our own self, other selves, and our wider environment. Perhaps this explains the naive 'vibes' and 'chemistry' so beloved of modern psychologically aware people. It is through the resonances of ch'i that we become sensitive to others' auras, movements and manners, and pick up intuitive information. It is through ch'i that synchronicity occurs, and divination through the I Ching is made possible. It is when the currents of ch'i are harmoniously integrated, or are encouraged to be, that its benefits arise.

Because the currents of ch'i within the human frame are of such importance to him in the fields, for instance, of the arts and acupuncture, it is not surprising that much study has gone into the forms which ch'i may take. Although the unitary nature of traditional ch'i never changes, this one bipolar multi-faceted energy exhibits itself not only in coarse and subtle forms, but in sub-varieties within each of them.

So it is that the subtle vitality which the ancient Taoists specifically identified by the name Ch'i is now only one among a number of classes of ch'i. Now called *wei ch'i*, it remains the invisible protective and defensive energy of the body and is diffused throughout the body, where it warms the flesh, regulates the pores, maintains the complexion, and protects bones and joints. It manifests itself as a layer of warm atmosphere on the skin's surface — the aura — and circulates throughout the meridian system and around all organs, muscles, and bones.

Distinct from wei ch'i is another subtle form called *yuan ch'i*. This is said to determine the individual's life span. It aids in the transformation of food into essential energy, known as *ku ch'i*. It is centred in the lower *tan t'ien*.

These are three examples of subtle bodily ch'i.

Coarser ch'i is represented by, for instance, *yeng ch'i*, which appears as the visible liquid energies that circulate through the blood vessels, the lymph glands, and the endocrinal glandular system.

Similarly, *ching ch'i* signifies the essential reproductive energy of the body. It is said to mature in young girls at the age of fourteen, and in boys at the age of sixteen. After those ages, should there be insufficient ching ch'i, the activities of coarse yeng ch'i and subtle wei ch'i decrease, leaving the body undernourished and prey to disease.

There are many other forms of bodily ch'i, each with its own function. They include *chen ch'i*, known as the healthy, physical vitality or physical essence, and *chung ch'i*. The latter is a good example of the depths of subtlety of observation achieved by Chinese scientist-mystics. They found that it is produced by ku ch'i having been sent to the lungs, where it is heated by the upper burner (of which more will be read in Chapter Seven). The resulting essence blends with the essence of heaven from the air. The resulting blend of these is then acted upon by yuan ch'i and further refined into chen ch'i.

In the same way, the ch'i of heaven and earth, once presumably regarded as identical to what became known as the bodily wei ch'i, has similarly been subdivided and categorized. For instance there are the two subtle ch'i, *ti ch'i* and *tien ch'i*. Ti ch'i is 'earth' or 'host' ch'i and is found in dragon veins. Tien ch'i is 'heaven' or 'guest' ch'i. As a guest, and as emanating from heaven, tien ch'i may of course overrule ti ch'i.

In any conflict, it is always possible for the coarser weather ch'i, five in number, to try to achieve harmony, in keeping with their association with the Five Elements.

Similarly, it is always possible for man to try to aim for harmony between heaven and earth, since such harmony has a bearing on his own fortunes. Man's ch'i is always greatly influenced by earth's (and heaven's) ch'i. The land influenced by earth's ch'i, for instance, most nearly brushing the surface of the earth is that which is believed to be the most habitable. If ch'i recedes too far beneath the surface, no water flows, pollution and sickness thrive, and there will be bad luck. Thus most of the *raison d'être* of *feng shui* practitioners is their supposed ability to direct smooth beneficial ch'i to clients, and to divert hectic, harmful ch'i from them.

Ch'i, despite the fact of extensive categorization, is a unity. Taoist practice, whether meditational, medicinal or martial, has always been based on a view of man as a microcosm, reflecting the macrocosmic universe. So much so, that human physical characteristics and functions have always been seen to have cosmic equivalents.

Heaven has four seasons and man has four limbs; heaven has five elements and so man has five internal organs; heaven has nine divisions, and man has nine orifices. A year has 360 days, therefore man has to have 360 joints. Heaven has wind, rain, cold and heat, so man has joy, anger, taking and giving.[6] Earth has dragon veins, just as man has meridians to channel the ch'i.

Thus the wise man seeks to move with the cosmic forces at least by analogy. He seeks to control change by aligning himself with the cosmic change born of and by the winds of ch'i.

2.

Change

To us, as much as to primitive man, the universe may often appear to be arbitrary.

Everything is in constant flux. Yet it is not a chaotic flux: it is change that is subject to laws. It therefore has meaning. Such laws include: the law of cause and effect, the law that all things and events are interrelated, and the law of recurrent change.

The presence of laws means that change can be predicted and possibly controlled. This is what the Chinese, in common with all other men, have been set on doing. They are no different in this from any other people, though their methods and resulting world view may of course be different. Where some prefer to shelve the matter, to place themselves perhaps in the everlasting arms of an omniscient and omnipotent God, the Chinese Taoists became scientist-mystics.

The law of cause and effect sometimes means that an effect can be precisely forecast from a cause: an object will fall earthwards when released, for instance. Yet no one (can they?) can say exactly where it will fall, or what configuration it will take up. Perhaps such knowledge would be possible if everything were known about the object: if the entire history of the universe were taken into account. There are, too, examples of seeming acausality which, in spite of no obvious causal connection between events, have meaning and are recognized in Chinese theory and practice.

An oft repeated statement in this book is that the Chinese have been scientists from the earliest times. The dictionary definition of science refers to the search for understanding and meaning and the formulation of laws. Such a search is necessary if only for men to escape the horror of living in a meaningless universe. This has led to the search for regularities, with resulting predictive power and ability to control.

As a result, Chinese scientist-mystics have formulated certain laws that explain the universe as they see it. Primarily they see the universe in its manifest form as an interconnected whole, as in Indra's net, each object reflecting the nature of each other object, each phenomenon partaking of the nature of all other phenomena.

One law that results from this is the law of harmony: that the universe is held together by the tension between positive and negative forces, between yin and yang. Without their constant interplay, the universe would collapse. Such interplay is at work in the earth and in man, in the whole man and in his parts. The search for harmony in conduct and in the environment has consequently been a constant preoccupation of the Chinese. Only thus can a man aid the process of resolving the tension and ensure the continuance of the universe of which he is a member.

This yin and yang law runs parallel to the other great law; the law, observed in nature, that change is cyclic: that all manifestations undergo a regular cycle of birth, growth, decay and death, whether they be bacteria, men and women, plants, mountains, stars or galaxies. To illustrate this principle, Taoists devised the Theory of the Five Elements. Its application enables Chinese to moderate the process of ineluctable change in themselves and in their environment.

Both yin and yang and the Theory of the Five Elements are aspects of ch'i, the ultimate material essence of the cosmos.

Yin and yang
Yin and yang are the cement of the manifest world, for it is they that maintain it in being. From the centrifugal force of the speed of the moon in space being balanced by the force of its mother earth's gravity, through all humans and human organizations, to the maintenance of the structure of an atom by balance and harmony, in all of these is seen the play of yin and yang.

The Su-wen says:

> Yin/yang is the Way of heaven and earth, the fundamental principle of the myriad things, the father and mother of change and transformation, the root of inception and destruction.

The Tao Te Ching says:

All things are backed by shade (yin) and faced by light (yang) and harmonized by the immaterial breath (ch'i).

Two of the principles to do with yin and yang laid down by the Yellow Emperor 2000 years before Christ, are, firstly, that all beings and things in the universe are aggregates of ch'i and are composed of varying proportions of yin and yang, and, secondly, that all beings and things are in a state of dynamic change, tension, and transformation which is unceasing. Man's place is to aid the processes of harmony: indeed it is to his advantage so to do.

Yin is represented by the symbol ▬ ▬, while yang is represented by ▬▬▬. Yin is static; yang is dynamic. Yin signifies endurance; yang signifies change. While yang may be said to be vital and positive, yin is that which encourages the maintenance of present states. So, in the human body, for instance, runaway yang, the power of the positive, would lead to uncontrolled expansion and rapid death, as would uncontrolled yin, the influence of the negative, through contraction and torpidity. The two need each other in the sense that neither could exist without the other, any more than any aspect of the world of the ten thousand things could exist without them: there is no light without dark, no death without life, no negative without positive, no man without woman, no creation without destruction.

Nothing can exist without its opposite: this is a fundamental truth: good needs evil if good is to be known as good.

Thus nothing in the cosmos can exist without the constant interplay of the two: ch'i, manifesting in the tension between yin and yang, is the 'Subtle Origin of all manifest beings and things. . .'[1]

All 'manifest beings' then, are subject to yin and yang: any destruction of the harmonious tension between the two will be destructive to beings, objects, systems, and empires either in the short or the long term. Not only do men and women need to subject themselves to the law, they need to seek to exemplify and increase the possibility of harmony between opposites, for all opposites partake of the nature of yin and yang. This is wisdom, the lifestyle of the Taoist Sage, the Confucian Superior Man.

So, in their gardens, such beings sought to have yin valleys and water balanced by yang hills and sky, sunlight by shadow, height by depth, and warmth by coolness.

They grew the lotus in their garden ponds, for, as Cooper has it,

It is both yin and yang and contains within itself the balance of the

Two Powers; it is solar, as blooming in the sun, and lunar, as rising from the dark of the waters of the pre-cosmic chaos. As the combination of air and water, this symbolizes spirit and matter. Its roots bedded in the darkness of the mud, depict indissolubility; its stem, the umbilical cord of life, attaches man to his origins and is also a world axis...[2]

In this plant is epitomized the interconnectedness of things: the presence in each of the qualities of all others, to be searched for and encouraged whenever and wherever possible. In the gardens of the Sage was found a continual attempt to increase the likelihood of harmony, to seek the interconnectedness of all things, and so the continuance of the universe of which man was a part.

Even the two indigenous philosophies of China, Taoism and Confucianism, partake of this interplay: Taoism supplying the mystic, artistic and creative aspects of life, and Confucianism supplying the ritual, the decorous and the niceties of social order. These opposites each played their part in the life of the people and helped to maintain balance.

The Five Elements
Such tensions arising from a mutual interplay of forces over every aspect of creation may arrive at a balance, but are unlikely in themselves to lead to any linear progression of evolutionary processes. In any case, the concept of evolution in the Darwinian sense, does not figure largely in Chinese thinking. They believe, relaxedly, in creation as following in all its aspects, cyclic patterns, regularities, and periodic returns to the source. As Chapter 25 of the Tao Te Ching has it, 'Going on means going far; going far means returning'.

Such a cyclic path will exhibit phases, and we come to the Theory of the Five Elements, *Wu Hsing*.

The five phases of energy evolution, earth, metal, water, wood, and fire, encompass all the phenomena of nature. It is a symbolism that applies itself equally to all life. (Su Wen)

The five elements are, of course, not confined to themselves, nor are they entirely representative of the underlying theoretical framework. They are symbols. Not only do they 'encompass all' phenomena, they also, in fact, include all substances or phenomena which share with them their basic characteristics. For instance, the element earth will include all phenomena that are to do with growth, and the element water will include all phenomena which share its characteristic of flowing downwards. So the five elements provide the Chinese with a complete means of explaining change and with a powerful tool with which to control change while at the same time maintaining a yin/yang balance.

As Ni, Hua Ching puts it,

> The five phases of energy evolution provide a complete philosophical and practical system which explains complex universal interrelations, and can be applied to reestablish disturbed energy arrangements and avoid conflicting situations.

That this concept is indeed a wide reaching one, involving a wide spectrum of human activity and applying to all of life, may be seen from Table 1.

Table 1

	Fire	Metal	Wood	Earth	Water
Organs	Heart	Lungs	Liver	Stomach	Bladder
	Small Intestine	Large Intestine	Gall-Bladder	Spleen	Kidneys
Flavour	Bitter	Hot	Sour	Sweet	Salty
Sense	Taste	Smell	Sight	Touch	Hearing
Colour	Red	White	Green	Yellow	Black
Emotion	Joy	Sadness	Anger	Reminiscence	Fear
Voice	Laughter	Crying	Shouting	Singing	Groaning
Energy	Directing	Physical	Psychic	Primal	Creative
Climate	Heat	Dryness	Wind	Humidity	Cold
Negative Drive	Greed	Stubborn	Hostility	Ambition	Desire
Mental Attributes	Spiritual	Sentimental	Rational	Tranquil	Desire
Morality	Humility	Rectitude	Benevolence	Trusting	Wisdom

Using the table, such a cycle can be quite simply illustrated by Figure 1.

From this, one can trace the cycle of, for instance, the emotions from joy to reminiscence to sadness to fear to anger and thence to joy again.

On the other hand, clearly, uncontrolled creativity will destroy balance and harmony, so that a destructive order is necessary to regain balance: see Figure 2.

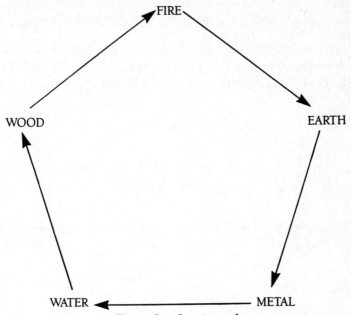

Figure 1: *Creative cycle*

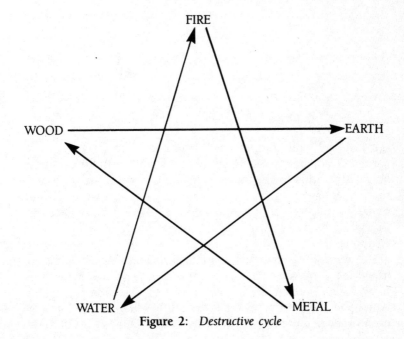

Figure 2: *Destructive cycle*

In this, joy destroys sadness, sadness destroys anger, anger destroys reminiscence, reminiscence destroys fear, and fear destroys joy.

Similarly, uncontrolled development of one of the elements will cause imbalance among the others, hence the need for what Ni, Hua-ching calls a competitive cycle: Figure 3.

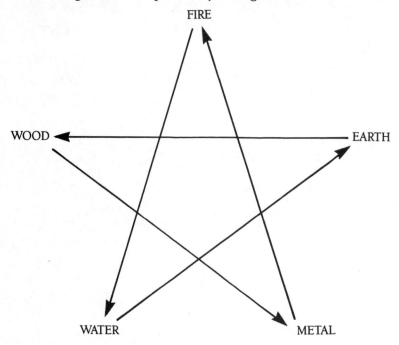

Figure 3: *Competitive cycle*

In this, joy will compete with fear, and so forth.

What is not clearly shown either in the table or in the diagrams, and which adds to the subtlety of the theory, is that each element may have a yin aspect or a yang aspect. As an example, the dynamic yang aspect of metal is killing, battle, purifying, changing, while its passive yin aspect signifies tools, implements and weapons.

The term 'Five Elements' may itself in fact be misleading for *hsing* (meaning 'to go') indicates movement, and so a better term might be, as Stephen Skinner points out, the 'Five Moving Agents', which, he says 'reinforces the idea that they generate and destroy each other in a continually moving cycle.'[3] This is true, perhaps, of the yang aspect, but not necessarily so for the yin.

Again, the term 'cycle' is a misleading one, if the reader is left with the impression of a cyclic movement progressing onward through time. First of all, this is because the concept of cyclic patterns is the antithesis of linear time marching inexorably to the future, and secondly, as we have seen, because the five elements (or agents) have at least three ways of interacting: creatively, destructively and competitively.

The I Ching

The avoidance of conflicting situations, which sums up Chinese scientific mysticism, is nowhere better exemplified than in the I Ching, the Book of Changes, sometimes called the Book of Transformations.

This is based on the yin ▬ ▬ and yang ▬▬▬, the Primeval Pair. These gave rise to the Four Forms: ▬ ▬, ▬▬▬, ▬▬▬ and ▬▬▬: the yin and yang in their two phases of static (the first two) and movable forms. From this arose the Eight Trigrams: ☰, ☱ ☲, ☳. ☴ ☵, ☶. ☷, and ☷.

> The Primeval Pair produce the Four Forms, from which are derived the Eight Trigrams... the Sages have seen the complexity of the universe. They used these symbols to represent the different forms and to symbolize their different characteristics.[4]

Each of the trigrams represents a force in nature, in either its passive, yin, aspect or its dynamic, yang, aspect. All phenomena in the universal flux, then, and their changes, could be represented by these trigrams. Of course, it was not to be expected that precise details of successive changes in particular cases would be vouchsafed, either from trigrams or from their successors, the sixty four hexagrams of the I Ching (Figure 4). Trends and tendencies were to be interpreted in following the rise and fall of the yin and yang. From these an experienced consultant could figure out the way to sail the ocean of flux in his or her life.

In using the I Ching to select the right hexagram for the purpose of divination, certain techniques involving the random fall of coins or yarrow stalks were evolved. Using these, the person consulting the oracle could be slotted into his present state of

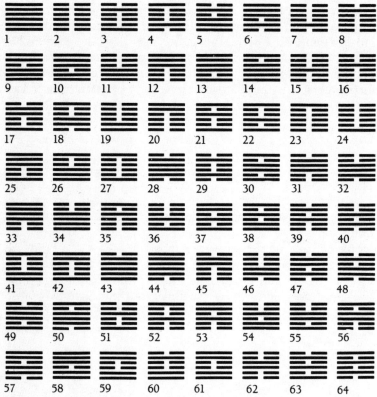

Figure 4: *The hexagrams in the order in which they appear in the I Ching*

energy response (ch'i) to the universe. Not only that, but the sort of change in his fortunes that were likely could also be foretold, depending on the fall of the sticks or coins. The randomness of the fall was assumed to be directly tied in with the question asked, and the state of mind and all the circumstances of the enquirer.

Conclusion

It is fairly easy to accept such a grand picture of change as that provided by the yin and yang. It is fairly easy to accept that the cycle of change can be as envisaged in some such schema as the Five Elements, or in the basic arrangement of the trigrams in the *Pa Gua* or the hexagrams in the I Ching. What is by no means so easy to accept by the Western mind is the belief that all these and especially divinatory methods such as the I Ching can be used as a tool to look at the minutiae of change in the life of a single individual.

If, however, we drop our Western tinted spectacles for a moment and accept as a working hypothesis that we humans are indeed an integral part of total creation, then certain consequences follow.

The obvious one (that is being borne in upon the West in spite of itself) is that the universe — or at any rate this minute speck, our planet — will soon sink or swim according to our actions. The alternative to that is that we will be forced to change by virtue of the yin/yang principle inherent in the universe. The change might be a drastic one.

A less obvious consequence is that certain events and phenomena at present largely inexplicable to the Western scientific mind may be less mysterious. For instance, as Ni, Hua-ching writes of the I Ching,

> The subtle spiritual energy formed by the person practising divination can cause the response of the universal energy which will give the appropriate answer... the coins, sticks... are extensions of the mind which vibrate the subtle energy network and receive the answer through the principle of energy response.

Psychic phenomena such as clairvoyance and telepathy are more easily understood, even if they are not fully explained, by this reference to the ch'i. If we humans are indeed parts of the universe, we are also parts of one another — one with each other — and it is then not impossible to envisage the possibility of communicating with one another over space and time. After all, genes communicate over time, and body cells communicate over space. If this is so in the microcosm, may it not be so in the macrocosm? We then may accept the possibility of communication with inanimate objects such as yarrow stalks. The individual consciousness is set aside in favour of a universal consciousness, whose vehicle is ch'i, just as the cell's consciousness, using the same vehicle, is set aside in favour of the body's.

3.

Setting Ch'i in Context

Taoism, Confucianism, and Buddhism were the three great religions of China. Taoism and Confucianism were indigenous, Buddhism an import. Thus Confucianism and Taoism shared many basic beliefs — or appeared to do so.

Confucianism

Confucianists and Taoists had a common belief in the existence of ch'i. A Confucianist wrote:

> Within the area of heaven and earth there is the yin ch'i and the yang ch'i, permanently filling and permeating men as water fills and permeates the fish in it, that which constitutes the difference between water and ch'i being that one is visible and the other invisible. . . although it appears to be nothing, yet it is something. Man is permanently imbued with this stream of the two ch'i.[1]

We may look to Chu Hsi, a Confucian of the twelfth century, to indicate the ways in which Confucianist beliefs in ch'i differed from those of the Taoists. Though he taught that ch'i was 'vital substance', he also taught that ch'i was itself subject to a higher ordering principle known as *li*, which controlled the various forms in which the ch'i might manifest. These forms were what made sense of the world, and the principle could be discerned in the classics, in nature, and in government. It was the task of men and women to seek to discern their own ordering principle, and those in the world around them, and, by strict adherence to ritual and symbolism, to seek to realize those principles in Yin and Yang (and therefore ch'i).[2]

The importance attached by Confucianists to li turned their system to an ethical pursuit, compared to the metaphysical bent of Taoism.

To Confucianists, it was property, ritual, ceremony and social order that kept the cosmos together: they were the directing principles behind ch'i, and ch'i was the force through which those properties (subsumed under the name li) were made manifest. The result in every day life was patriarchal human relations in which filial piety was the supreme virtue (leading to a tendency to submit to authority). The Superior Man was the ideal human, devoted to worship of the ancestor, to guiding his life according to the Golden Mean.

In short, Confucianism represented the yang side of Chinese life: patriarchal, sober, ambitious (through a system of public examinations based on Confucian teachings) and practical. Propriety, ritual ceremony and social order were to Confucianists the cement that kept the cosmos in being: they were the directing forces that controlled the flow of ch'i. Rationality and forethought were at a premium, though, of course, an outsider may discern the seed pearl of their opposite always visible in the unthinking observance of rites.

There is much fruitless discussion as to whether Lao Tzu and Confucius were contemporaries. What is more interesting is the way in which their systems illustrate in China the very belief in the yin and the yang that is fundamental to both belief-systems.

Confucianism, if it can be called a religion at all, is very puritanical. A Confucian Temple would display but a single tablet to Confucius in an otherwise bare room. Compared with popular Buddhism and, especially, popular Taoism, with its pantheon of gods and magical rites, this was stark indeed. So too must the ethical and social system that went with Confucianism have seemed to the ordinary man and woman with their belief in spirits, and their need to placate the spirits.

Yet Confucius himself, if we look to his sayings as recorded in 'The Analects', was a cheerful man, in life-style not so very far removed from that of the Taoist.

In late spring, after the spring clothes have been newly made, I should like, together with five or six adults and six or seven boys, to go bathing in the River Yi and enjoy the breeze on the Rain Altar and then go home chanting poetry. . .
   In the eating of coarse rice and the drinking of water, the using

of one's elbow for a pillow, joy is to be found. Wealth and rank attained through immoral means have as much to do with me as passing clouds.[3]

So spake Confucius in his lifetime, about 500 BC. One thousand years later, the system which he founded had become heavily circumscribed, as we have seen, with ritual so heavy that any burgeoning of the free spirit would have been impossible (or so it would seem to us in our age).

Even two hundred years after his lifetime, Chuang Tsu, described by some as the greatest Taoist, was already ridiculing him and his followers. In Chapter 32 of the Chuang Tzu book, he says, 'Confucius is a man of outward show and of specious words. He mistakes the branch for the root.'[4] In this passage, no doubt, Chuang Tzu is referring back to the words in the opening chapter of the Tao Te Ching: 'The name that can be named is not the unchanging name'. He believed that Confucius and his followers mistook the manifest aspects of the Tao for the eternal, unnameable Tao.

The difference between Confucius the man and what was made of him by his followers is an extreme case of what so often happens to great people. In Confucianism of the later period, there appears to be little of the spirit of its founder. That this fate has not overcome Taoism to anything like the same degree, is a matter for remark and thanks.

Later Confucianism depended upon the thinking enshrined in the classics: the Shu Ching, a collection of historical documents; the Shih Ching, poems; Li Chi, a book of rites and ceremonies, upon which Confucianists relied to an extreme; the I Ching, the divinatory Book of Changes; and the Annals of Lu.

From these classics derived ideas that covered all eventualities that man might meet in his life time, to do with cosmology, political government, social organization and individual conduct.

Confucianism represents the practical, sober, social side of Chinese life. It was a system of social, moral and political order based on the impeccable conduct of the Superior Man. The Confucian system involved him in ritual and proper deportment. Every movement the Superior Man made was a ritual, everything he did or wore was symbolic:

The robe worn by the scholar-gentleman was in itself a moral symbol. The roundness of the sleeves represented the manners in the elegance and perfection of the circle. The straightness of the seams depicted justice and incorruptibility. . .'[5]

Socially it was faultless conduct and courtesy which always put others before oneself; historically and politically it implied an ideal order and a rigid self-discipline.

While the Confucian Superior Man and the Taoist Sage are some-times treated as indistinguishable, they are in fact very different, and in themselves serve to point out the obvious differences between the two systems. Mencius said that 'The Superior man cultivates a friendly harmony without being weak . . . stands erect without leaning to one side or the other. He does not treat with contempt his inferiors, nor court the favours of his superiors'. The Taoist Sage, on the other hand, cultivates nothing (No-thing: a faint echo of the Buddhist concept of the Void). He is content to practise *wu-wei* (anathema to Confucianists), to study the manifestations of change around and in him, and attempt to go with their flow.

As we shall see in Chapter 11, questions of moral imperatives do not arise with him, because the only imperative is to be in tune with the yin and yang, cultivating the flow of ch'i, the cos-mic energy which should not be opposed.

The differences between Taoism and Confucianism are foreseen in the First Chapter of the Tao Te Ching:

> The Tao that can be expressed is not the eternal Tao:
> The name that can be defined is not the unchanging name.
> Non-existence is called the antecedent of heaven and earth;
> Existence is the mother of all things.
> From eternal non-existence, therefore, we serenely observe the mysterious beginning of the Universe;
> From eternal existence we clearly see the apparent distinctions.

It would seem that Chuang Tzu was right when he criticized Confucianists for seeing li as defining and limiting what could not be defined or limited, and basing their whole system on that, to Taoists, fundamental error.

It is easy to see that Taoism, at its best a metaphysical, mysti-cal, light-hearted and artistic way of life, represented a complete contrast to Confucianism; it was the yin of society, counterbalanc-ing the yang of Confucianism. While, since they were human sys-tems, the two systems were often at odds, they nevertheless provided a solid underpinning to the fabric of Chinese life. The debate between them can be seen as the interplay of the two forces, never ending, but always in a dynamic tension and balance. Each learnt from the other, as in the way the ten Commentaries by Confucius on the I Ching opened up its mysteries to Taoist mystics.

Buddhism
Where does Buddhism fit into the purely Chinese systems described do far?

It is not necessary to describe Buddhism in detail, even if that were humanly possible in this context. Suffice it to say that when it came across the mountains from India, it did fill a void, and even successfully vied with Confucianism, by then the State Religion.

Buddhism, in its popular forms, held much in common with most native religions it met on its proselytizing trips abroad. One common belief was faith in prayer to minor deities, which it saw as efficacious means to an individual's final enlightenment. In this, it was able to meet with popular Taoism, in whose temples a pantheon of gods was to be found (not strange in a religion that saw ch'i, the emanation of Tao, as visible in all material phenomena).

But our concern is with ch'i, and that is a concept quite foreign to Buddhism. Even today there are fundamental differences between Buddhism and both Taoism and Confucianism. Apart from the Buddha's professed unconcern with any Final Cause, and thus with his followers' lack of curiosity about God, Tao, ch'i, or anything other than with the four noble truths of suffering, its cause, its remedy, and the method to achieve the remedy, there was also the fundamental difference between them in the concept of and belief in reincarnation.

Where the Chinese systems saw one life only as the lot of every man and woman, and therefore spent much time and effort in seeking to prolong this life, Buddhism bases itself on the belief of its motherland, India, that this life is but one of a series leading finally to extinction in Nirvana. It is interesting to note that the Chinese Taoists saw an immortality arising from a merging with the cosmos as a desirable end to their one life. In this, the final goals are similar, but the means and underlying belief-systems are very different.

So what had Buddhism to offer the Chinese? There is little doubt that the idea of reincarnation holds a fascination for everyone, not least for a people that had been led to believe that they had only one bite at the cherry of life. In particular, the Pure Land sect of Buddhism held out a promise of a blissful paradise for believers (similar in many respects to the Christian Heaven).

At the same time, pure Taoism had much to offer Buddhism.

Ch'an Buddhism

Buddhism, presumably proselytizing, entered China, as we have seen, in the first century AD. It was badly received at first, perhaps because of the ritual mendicancy of the monks. But by the sixth century many of the Indian schools were well established, and were no doubt adding to the existing yin/yang tensions between the high-minded codes of Confucianism and the complementary freedom of Taoism. Chinese religion reached a low point, losing its way between the spiritual barrenness of Confucianism, and the philosophical fecundity of Indian Buddhism. At first sight, Indian Buddhism and Confucianism might be thought to have a lot in common: both were concerned with man as an active agent in taming and channelling his own nature. The Confucians saw conformity with li as the ideal way to perfection; the Buddhists saw control of the mind as that path. But compared to the rich complexity of developed Buddhist psychology, Confucianism had little to offer on the intellectual side, no hope to offer on the metaphysical.

Somewhere around, like an underground river, was Taoism. One can envisage the latter, its followers always emulating water, flowing easily along and forming watercourses amongst the hard opposing rocks of Confucianism and Indian Buddhism.

The Taoist attitude was the reverse of both: uninterested in ethics, believing that right behaviour sprang spontaneously from the exigencies of the moment, and in respect of the workings of the mind, by 'action in inaction' (wu wei) to overcome obstacles which are in fact merely a product of the mind. There was thus in the latter a secret growth point between Taoism and Buddhism which was lacking between Confucianism and Buddhism.

Indeed, Taoism has been described as the most mystical of religions: it could be argued that it had much to teach the Budd-hists of that era (corresponding roughly to the opening years of Christianity). By that time the Buddhists were weighed down in philosophical and psychological enquiry, and, for ordinary prac-titioners, it was doubtless getting too forested to see any trees, or even a way through the forest to the slopes of the mountain.

Buddhist travellers found that Taoism was mystically respectable, not out of touch with reality in the earthly or transcendental sense, and therefore was acceptable as a possible way forward.

Sometime, then, around the sixth or seventh century, there occurred an amalgam of Taoism and Buddhism, the result being commonly called Ch'an Buddhism.

In this amalgam, Taoism was the loser.

How and why the amalgam happened is not clear.

Buddhism had come across the mountains from India laden with an enormous psychological/philosophical system, which had been produced over centuries by India's best and most exquisitely meticulous intellectuals. Such a system needs, from time to time, streams of new thinking, otherwise there is a danger of petrification. Like a fresh mountain torrent, Taoism provided a way of cutting through that rock barrier.

But it was an Indian Buddhist, by name Bodidharma, who made that breakthrough: it was he who crashed through the rocks. Like a torrent that has been dammed and then released, Ch'an Buddhism appeared with Bodidharma in about the six century AD. It was he who arrived in China and made common cause with the cloud-like simplicity of Taoism.

The Ch'an school of Buddhism that emerged was a protest at the second-hand approach to Truth of the existing Buddhist schools. It brought a new and unique insistence on direct, immediate advance to Reality. It provided means to a 'direct existential grasp of reality'.

There is no doubt that Ch'an Buddhists of the T'ang period (c. AD 7-10) were inheritors of the thought and spirit of Chuang Tzu and Lao Tzu.

The word 'Ch'an' comes from the same root as the Sanskrit 'dhyana', meaning something like 'deep meditation', and stories of Bodidharma spending seven years of his life facing a wall in meditation give something of the flavour of the man, to be set beside his habit of appearing before Personages clad in rags. Not much is known of him, but he appears to have been quite close, in personal life-style and in approach to others, to the Taoist Sage, the 'complete man' of Chuang Tzu. He had a disregard of social niceties and personal advancement. He surely had contact with the Taoist classics, with the works at least of Lao Tzu and Chuang Tzu.

He would have appealed to Chuang Tzu, and indeed he would certainly have found Chuang Tzu's writings much to his liking, and the kind of thought and culture represented by the latter transformed the highly speculative and ratiocinative Indian Buddhism into the meditative kind of Buddhism represented by the seventh century Flower Ornament School of Ch'an Buddhism, from which the Zen arts of flower arranging are doubtless descended.

Japanese (and therefore Western, Beat) Zen Buddhism is the direct descendant of Chinese Ch'an Buddhism.

What of the Tao, and ch'i?

Spontaneity of action is the ideal both of Zen and of Taoism. In Zen it is only acquired by undergoing a severe training, 'as ruled and fettered as the result is free'. This seems a long way from Chuang Tzu's advice to sit and breathe through one's heels, from his dislike of formality. As Ruth Fuller Sasaki indicated in her ordination as a Zen priest in 1958, Zen has moved far from those ideals and methods. She said: 'In the Western world Zen seems to be going through the cult phase. Zen is not a cult. The problem with Western people today is that they want to believe in something and at the same time they want something easy. Zen is a lifetime work of self-discipline and study'. This is a far cry indeed from the easy flow through life of the Taoist Sage.

Zen Buddhism developed in Japan from, and no doubt in reaction to, Chinese Ch'an in the same way as Ch'an developed in reaction to Indian Buddhism. Each people brings its own flavour and approach to Buddhism, just as Buddhism brings its own flavour to indigenous religions. What it had brought to Taoism was a psychological emphasis upon the workings of the mind.

It was a route that led in its own way to self-realization, but it was a route that was not Taoist.

Ch'an took the Buddhist path and in doing so lost the Taoist view of the world as a living organism with man an integral part of it, in favour of personal salvation or universal compassion, arahatship or bodhisattvahood. It lost sight of its own, older path to the mountain peaks, of its own, older roots, those that involve a knowledge of yin/yang, of cyclic change and ch'i.

So Taoism as a philosophy and a way of life has gone its own way in China, remaining much as it began: a Way, a Tao, that turns its back on organization, on untoward striving, remaining dynamically organic and cosmos centred.

What is remarkable is that such a self-effacing Way has survived so well in the face of the big battalions, and has managed, as we shall see, to contribute much to so many fields of practical human endeavour.

4.

The Grassroots: Taoist Magic

> Magick has led the world from before the beginning of history, if only for the reason that Magick has always been the mother of Science.[1]

This quotation reflects a view that magic investigates the laws of nature with the idea of making use of them, a definition not so very far from a Western definition of science itself. 'Science, *n*. knowledge; knowledge ascertained by observation and experiment, critically tested, systematized and brought under general principles. . .' (*Chambers Twentieth Century Dictionary*).

Implicit in Western science is the notion that nature exists to be plundered.

Taoism and eastern philosophies without exception take the view that such plundering affects the whole, that man is not separate from nature when he does things to it, extracts things from it. On the contrary he is an integral part of nature, and everything he does, he does to himself.

It is clear, therefore, that as an Eastern view of science will differ fundamentally from the twentieth-century Western view, so perhaps will a Chinese view of magic.

The Chambers dictionary definition of magic is:

> the art of produing marvellous results by compelling the aid of spirits, or by using the secret forces of nature, such as the power residing in certain objects as 'givers of life'; enchantment; sorcery; art of producing illusions by legerdemain; a secret or mysterious power over the imagination or will.

This again is a western definition which clearly seeks to differentiate between science and magic. Yet it has been said that magic is in fact 'science in the tentative stage', and this is a view that would no doubt be accepted by sorcerers everywhere, certainly by the Chinese variety.

Ch'i is in itself open to magic, since it is a secret force of nature. Dragon veins and acupuncture meridians, T'ai Chi and talismans, all partake of the magical — and of the scientific. All have been the useful result of systematic investigation. Just as science evolves its own technology, it is certainly not far from the truth to say that a technology emerged from the study of ch'i, putting the early tentative findings to very tentative practical use in everyday life until confidence was gained over the centuries.

This chapter will be concerned much with the art (or technology) of magic as it involves control of ch'i, and not very much with the compelling of spirits — insofar as the two can be separated. This is not easy, for even Taoist doctors who relied on medicinal talismans and the invoking of Spirits of the Prior Heavens as a major part of their cures still took care to situate their surgeries by means of observing feng shui geomantic signs, and these, as we shall see, rely upon the ch'i of the Earth. Ch'i is all pervasive. It also comes in various forms, some more subtle than others.

Magic was always an integral part of Taoist practice, if only because their world view was so wide and took in all of human experience. As Da Liu says, '. . .Taoist physicians travelling about the Chinese countryside used many methods with genuine curative value in their treatment of diseases, but also used magic spells, which had the advantage of costing nothing to practice.'[2]

Spells had a hold on the minds of Chinese, as indeed, they do on the minds of even modern man: early Chinese history has a host of stories illustrating the power of spells and sorcery. The use of relatively coarse ch'i is mentioned in the Pao-p'u tzu as a method of casting spells. By rendering his breath more abundant, the Taoist Chao Ping was said to have charmed streams so that the water level dropped as much as twenty feet. Using the same technique he would light a cooking fire on thatched roofs without setting light to the dwelling, render boiling water harmless for scalding and prevent dogs from barking.[3]

Yet it would be foolish to say that the use of spells by sorcerers of any culture is not based on some process of rational thought and experimentation. Even in the most extreme of magical tales a trace of a rational basis for Chinese magic can often be seen. For example, one of the greatest of sorcerers, Yu the Great, who did so much magic to save China from the ravages of a great flood in about 2350 BC, is nevertheless reputed to have paid great attention to the theory of the Five Elements which sought to explain and therefore control change in general.

In Taoism, the human body, like the world and the cosmos, is 'permeated by energies'. These pass through it from outside, 'sweeping its doings, thoughts and histories along in their progress'. Yet man is a conscious being, and can hope to control the energies. For instance, the Pao-p'u tzu states:

> Man exists in ch'i, and ch'i is within man himself. From Heaven and Earth to all kinds of creation, there is nothing which would not require ch'i to stay alive. The man who knows how to circulate his ch'i maintains his own person *and also banishes evils that might harm him.*[4]

Magical practices, then, including the use of charms and talismans, were based on a recognition of the power of ch'i, one of 'the secret forces of nature'. Magicians provided magic in order to influence the Five Elements, which were recognized to be manifestations of changing ch'i, that great ocean of vital power in which everything subsists. They did not hesitate to summon to earth during rituals the Five Primordial Spirits who dwell in the Prior Heavens: Fu Hsi for the East, Shen Nung for the South, Huang-ti for the Centre, Shao-hao for the West, and Chuan-hsu for the North. These spirit dignitaries were each accompanied by their spirit-ministers. All this ritual was closely connected with the science and technology associated with the workings of yin-yang and the Five Elements. There was of course another function for such goings-on. They brought to the minds of common folk the patterns of change which ruled them and of which they formed an integral part, and, therefore, the mystery of human existence.

It is only comparatively recently that men have seen themselves as fundamentally separate and distinct from the rest of creation, and have hubristically denied their membership of the cosmos.

Modern man is still a part of nature, yet because he recognizes himself as a uniquely conscious being with power to depart from nature, he separates himself from the cosmic process.

Yet how far can he go? He has been described by Jung as the 'unfinished creature' and he behaves as if this is so: always seeking as he does for a goal that the East would say he already has in his grasp. He is perhaps further from its realization than when he was able openly to declare his belief in spirits.

The goal in magical Taoism is what it is in all other Taoist practices. It is for each individual to reach that stage of spontaneity in action that comes with oneness with all of nature: with the universe itself. It is a state of being in which he takes 'no initiative to produce either happiness or disaster; he responds to each influence, and moves as he feels pressure, acting when he must', like a great tree possessed of consciousness and mobility.

Here is the need that the Taoists have always recognized, the need for man to go with the flow, to practice wu wei, letting go, to cease from striving and to cooperate fully with his nature, which is that of the Universe. As Chuang Tzu made Lao Tzu say to Confucius in an imaginary conversation: 'All this talk of charity and duty to one's neighbour drives me nearly crazy. Sir, strive to keep the world in its original simplicity and, as the wind bloweth wheresoever it listeth, so let virtue establish itself. Wherefore this undue energy, as though searching for a fugitive with a big drum?'

Yet it was necessary to satisfy the common man with the big drums of wonders and ritual if he was to be led to the beginning of the path that leads to the Immortals.

In a man, the practice of wu wei is, because it must be, a conscious process, nowhere better exemplified than by Alan Watts and others in their liking it to the actions of a skilled yachtsman who uses the forces of nature to move towards a goal. This is what animals may be observed to be doing: a cat stalking its prey in a shrubbery or a cow seeking shade in rough pastureland. There is a vast difference between these and the fatalistic acceptance shown by a cat in a vivisectionist's trap.

The whole apparatus of Taoist magic, mysticism and philosophy was devised for the express purpose of mapping approaches to this pinnacle of apparent simplicity.

Changes in the flow of ch'i are explained in the theory of the Five Elements. An appreciation of the Five Elements is similar to a knowledge of wind and sail: an alteration in one leads to a controllable change in the other and so to the achievement of the goal: in the case of Taoism, the everyday and final attainment of a peaceful and happy life.

In using the Five Elements, a magician needs to look at a person's destiny in both the long term and the short term.

As regards the long term, he believes that the 'energy arrangement' at the time of birth shapes the potential events of a person's life. Astrological considerations are thus important, and are based on the results of long research, based on centuries of experience.

Astrologers use a calendar system based on the constant repetition of a sixty-year or sixty-day cycle which has been used in China to mark out divisions in time since before 1000 BC. This is combined with consideration of a cycle of ten characters known as the Ten Heavenly Stems and another consisting of the Twelve Earthly Branches. By taking into consideration the cycles marking the client's year, month, day and hour of his birth, the Taoist occult expert is able to make a correlation with the Five Elements, and the symbols associated with them.

By calculating the five phases of energy evolution exhibited at the time of a person's birth, beneficial or inauspicious times can be determined. This information can help the individual to plan his life. By understanding the cycles of his life and of the universe, he can, in theory, know the right time for any action, decision or enterprise.

The magician thus has a useful knowledge of astrology. This gives him insight into the life pattern of his client, and he is thus able to help in the short term, in problems related to health, relationships, and life crisis points like birth, marriage and death. In all of these, a knowledge of the phasing of change according to the Five Element theory and a consequent controlling of the flow of ch'i can make things go well for the client.

Sex, for instance, plays a large part in the lives of most people, and has long been regarded as a vehicle by which ch'i may be channelled to one or both of the participants' advantage. But it is not only to the couple's advantage, it is also to the advantage of the Universe as a whole, since it is believed that the union of female and male, negative and positive, yin and yang, leads to the harmony of the Universe. Taoists believe that Heaven and Earth consummate their relation each time a man and a woman perform the sexual act.

It is interesting, in this regard, to note that there was, in pre-Buddhist days, a Taoist ritual known as the 'deliverance from guilt' ceremony on new moon and full moon nights. This consisted of a preliminary ritual dance, the 'coiling of the dragon and playing of the tiger', which ended in successive sexual unions among all participants.

Universal harmony is the constant aim, so that the prolongation of coitus, however and wherever performed, becomes a magic ritual. There are lucky and unlucky days for intercourse, easily calculated from the birth signs. Similarly, advice could be given on favourable directions in which to lie and so on.

Taoist everyday magic relies much on astrology and the Five Element theory. The Five Elements, wood, fire, earth, metal and water, besides having characteristics of their own which are reflected in individual's psychic make-up, have associated with them not only spirits of the five directions, but symbols of all kinds, including symbolic colours, each of which is related to others according to the cycles of mutual growth and decay of the Five Elements. For instance, wood has blue as its associated colour, while water has black, and metal, white.

This means that once a person's dominant element has been found, the cycle of development may be used to enhance it by means of the use of colour in clothing or home. For example, people with wood dominant in their psychic make-up are recommended to wear black (symbolic of water) in order to nourish it. White (symbolic of metal) should be avoided, since it will clearly be able to cut down the wood, and with it the person's luck. There is a clear recognition here of the potential use of magic against people.

Such examples illustrate the belief that men and women are able to influence the processes of the Universe by magical participation in them rather than by succumbing to fatalistic acceptance.

The theory of the Five Elements, at least, appears to offer to men and women a means whereby the cosmic pattern of change can be detected and then influenced by acts of sympathetic magic when taken in conjunction with birth dates and so forth.

Of course, magic can be debased. It is difficult, for instance, to relate the following examples to much more than a passing knowledge of the Five Elements. The cures appear to partake more of faith-healing or mere common sense.

An imbalance of wood, for instance, could be corrected by giving the bed three or four shakes after getting up; for an imbalance of earth, the sufferer might be recommended to find a mole nearest their heart, rub moisturizer on it, and massage circularly for the number of years in their age. To balance fire, they should wear something cool, such as suede, silk or jade: this should be worn until their next birthday.

Similarly, shortages of a desired characteristic associated with an element may be increased by means of symbolic representations brought into daily life. For instance, a person short of characteristics of the element fire should perhaps keep an altar with an image of a fire god lit by a red electric light bulb; someone short of a characteristic of wood, should buy a wooden door or bed. If short of water (symbolic of money), it would be a good idea to put a fish bowl or water basin in the room. Someone short of earth, should stay close to the ground and not at the top of a high rise block of flats: they should pick a bungalow with foundations in the earth and have lots of pots around filled with earth and plants.[5]

Nevertheless, as suggested above, even such simple magic can serve to remind people of less evanescent verities.

Talismans

Another remedy used by magicians in helping their clients was the use of talismans. The dictionary defines these as objects 'supposed to be endued with magical powers: amulets, charms'.

Two million paper talismans are printed annually at New Year in China today. There are three thousand basic types and several hundred charts and diagrams. Even if it is now, with the sophisticated urbanite, at the level of a Westerner avoiding passing beneath a ladder, the ancient art seems to survive, certainly in rural areas. A millenium and a half ago, they were very common, being worn on the person, put on doors, corners, pillars, beams, set up at road junctions and other public spots.

Even in very recent times, the use of red, of waving banners, and good luck ideographs so beloved of Mao Tse Tung and his followers was a clear recognition by them of the power of such and similar symbols on the minds of ordinary people.

Talismans used, and still use, a strange calligraphy often known as 'cloud script' that has been handed down by ancient Taoist mystics. Sometimes the script is based on the dance steps taken by such Masters. The logic of this is clear: as an art of movement, dance symbolizes the principle of change.

The magic dance of the legendary limping emperor Yu is often referred to in talismanic compositions. These movements which were taught to Yu by heavenly spirits to give him command over the spirits of nature, originally represented a kind of hopping dance that Taoist shaman sorcerers often performed while in trance. But the Taoists were primarily concerned with the magic power of calligraphy, and

considered its effectiveness to lie above all in the line traced by the
sorcerer's feet in dance. . .[6]

On almost all the ancient talismans there will be found in the
upper 'celestial' half a vortex or spiral which represents the Cosmic energy, ch'i, which the talisman sought to appease and control.

Written characters were generally vertically arranged: this style
has survived in Chinese and Japanese hanging paintings to this day.

The material of which talismans were made varied widely. Some
were written on peach-wood plaques 6″ × 3″ in five colours, some
were written on paper or silk, while some were on jade or gold
tablets.[7]

These talismans were used, then, as another means of providing the sympathetic magic required to influence change through
the Five Elements. Besides the precise diagnostic skills required,
precise timing of the manufacture of the magic object was essential. This used the same skills and apparatus as was used to con-
struct the astrological birth chart mentioned above. Both these
circumstances combine to give what many might see as a scientific gloss to the enterprise. Certainly there is enough of the scientific about it to reinforce the definition of magic with which this
chapter started.

Here is an example, given in *Tao Magic* by Laszlo Legeza, of the
proper use of a talisman which was used to revitalize the eyes
and which contains references to this cyclic Five Element system. The instructions were that it was to be used under the sign
of the fourth branch (with corresponding symbolic animal Hare,
zodiacal sign Cancer, hours 5-7 am, point of compass East) and
the tenth branch (i.e., cock, Capricorn, 5-7 pm, West) of the Twelve
Earthly Branches, representing the ch'i of the radiance of the sun
and the moon.[8]

The choice of lucky and unlucky days, which features so promi-
nently in Chinese divination and farmers' almanacs is another
of the practical extensions of the yin-yang and Five Elements
theory.

I Ching
Another means by which people were able to get an inside look
at what the fates had in store, by slotting in, as it were, to the
state of changes current in their lives at any particular time, was

divination. There are many scores of divination methods, the best known in the West being the I Ching.

The very act of consulting the I Ching or any other divinatory system is, as in all other techniques that involve ch'i and its changes, a harmonizing act. It brings the mental world of the consulter into direct relationship with the pattern of energy currents in which he is immersed.

It is said that the original of the classic *The Secret of the Golden Flower*, translated for the West by Richard Wilhelm, was originally written entirely through divinatory methods, this time involving the tracing out of characters in sand by means of a suspended wand.

All divinatory methods succeed, it is said, to the extent that the consulter is tuned to the total situation, including most importantly the state of the universal energy net, ch'i. The art of mystical prediction is based on the universal law of energy response, principles of yin and yang and the five phases of energy evolution. All these, properly used, can reveal as yet unknown events and facts.

The Universal Energy ch'i will respond appropriately and naturally in integrating with the spiritual energy ch'i of the consulter. 'One may. . . say that the images have already taken form in the diviner's mind and the external system (yarrow stalks, coins, wands, etc.) merely develops the picture for the purpose of correct judgement.'[9]

There is little doubt, as we have seen, that there is a fair amount of gobbledegook in magic of all kinds. Much of a stage magician's success is due to the willingness of his audience to be fooled, just as much of the doctor's success is due to his patient's willingness to believe in his powers.

It is difficult to be sure how much of the success of talismans, for instance, is due to their actual efficacy in controlling the flow of ch'i and how much is due to such other factors.

Conclusion

It is clear that two aims are present in Chinese Taoist magic. The first of these is explicitly aimed at control of change. It makes use of magic rites and ritual activities, and these, with the use of talismans and charms, were aimed to win control of the changes that inevitably assail men and women as they followed the pathways of their lives. To the masses it must have seemed that Taoist masters were magicians: anyone who could identify himself with the energies of the universe should be able to control at least the more modest problems of human life.

But the spirit of philosophical Taoism remains the most important mystic ingredient in all Taoist practices. Therefore the second, implicit, aim of magical activities was to provide a link between popular mass-appeal Taoism and Taoist mysticism, and to harmonize sectarian views and esoteric teachings without discrediting either. It aimed to synthesize the New Year fire-crackers with the silence of the hermit's mountain home: both being recognized ways of spiritual communication.

5.

The Arts

. . . spend ten years observing bamboos, become a bamboo yourself, then forget everything and paint.[1]

In what way does ch'i manifest itself in Chinese art?

It is reasonable to start off from the premise that artists everywhere seek to understand their world, and to impose some form of meaning upon the chaos they observe. Art gives shape and meaning to life. It is not difficult to assume that cave paintings represent man's earliest attempts to control the forces of nature and the ten thousand things. It seems that man has always had an inkling or a hope that behind the manifestations of everyday life there lay a unifying principle of some kind.

He sought for harmony, not least in China. As we have seen in Chapter One, the visual arts in China can be traced back to early Taoist magical attempts to understand, control and predict.

Lao Tzu says, 'Tao begets one; one begets two; two begets three; three begets all things. The ten thousand things are begotten by Tao, but exist within Tao.'[2] There is therefore a potential available for understanding the harmony that underlies seeming chaos. In art, as in all other departments of their lives, Taoists sought that potential and resultant harmony.

Thus, although often concerned with scenes from nature, Chinese art and poetry have never been merely imitative. Consciously or unconsciously, artists and poets sought to reveal a deeper metaphysical content.

Chang Chung-yuan writes: 'In painting, Ch'i is that which reveals the objective reality of the form. In other words, Ch'i makes the painting exist for itself and moves it beyond itself. It is what Jacques Maritain calls "immanent action" in his exposition of creative intuition'. The action of the artist arises from within his conception of the universal.[3]

That sounds deep and heavy. If Taoism is anything, if artists are what they have always and everywhere been, it is not that. Cooper, for instance, writes,

> The artist did not go out to study nature, to use it as an escape and then return to his city studio at night; he lived with nature and was part and parcel of it. It was in no way external to him, something to soothe and delight, but it was his very being, he was wholly identified with the cosmic rhythms and harmony in a total awareness... Taoist art was entirely metaphysical, art was a mirror of the soul...[4]

Yet there was a lighter side to creativity. It is, at least, likely that Taoist and Zen artists were and are what artists have always been, rather more human. Alan Watts, not surprisingly or untypically, chooses to quote this picture of a Taoist painter at work:

> Chen Jung... was noted for the simplicity of his life and the competence with which he fulfilled his duties as a magistrate... Finally, he was admired for his habits of a confirmed drunkard. 'He made clouds by splashing ink on his pictures. For mists he spat out water. When wrought up by wine he uttered a great shout and, seizing his hat, used it for a brush, roughly smearing his drawing, after which he finished his work with a proper brush'[5]

As Bolen says, 'to experience the eternal Tao requires that our consciousness perceive through the workings of the right cerebral hemisphere, turning off the analytical, skeptical workings of the left...'[6] An artist, it could be argued, is only aware that certain idiosyncratic activities trigger access to the immanent, and is not afraid to use them. The spontaneity and unconventionality associated with Taoism would have made this easier for him.

However it is achieved, harmony, in art as in all aspects of Taoist living, is the target. Harmony is the resolution of opposites, and thus we are drawn to a fuller consideration of the yin and the yang.

Taoist Chinese art of all kinds is full of yang and yin, each balancing the other. Yang, being positive, active, male, penetrating, red and heavenly, is symbolized in painting and poetry by stallion, dragon, ram, cock, horned beasts, jade, mountain, summer and the south. Yin being negative, female, receptive, passive, dark and earthy, is symbolized by fungus, whirling shapes of cloud and water, valley, winter, north, vase, peach, female dragon, peony, fish and chrysanthemum. By placing such symbols in juxtaposition, Taoists hoped that each would influence and balance the other. It is the tension in these efforts that provides the strength in the works. In short, works of art were, in early times, especially, but not exclusively, made and used as practical magic. Their portrayals of harmony are meant to *induce* harmony.

For in Taoist art, as in yoga and health, the aim is harmony, and this means harmony between yin and yang. Such harmony is aimed at providing a *rapprochement* between humans and their chaotic and turbulent universe, of which they are much more an integral part than any bland Western acceptance of those words can imply.

Chang Chung-yuan quotes Hsuing Shih-Li who explains:

> that which is yin indicates form; that which is yang indicates spirit. Ten thousand things (the everyday world), all carrying a form and hiding a spirit, are in motion with the multitude. When yin and yang harmonize the ten thousand things are transformed. This is called the union of ch'i.[7]

Since it is a function of ch'i to unify the appearance (yin) with the reality (yang) of ten thousand things, it would appear that the artist who essays to do likewise should ally himself with the Universal Spirit in order to achieve this.

So in the composition of a picture, as much as in the trials of skill in Martial Arts, this interplay and balance of yin and yang will be seen most subtly in the use of light and dark, of space and non-space.

> Generally speaking, when the left side is vacant, the right side should be solid; when the right side is vacant, then the left side should be solid... White vacancy is yang or light; solid ink wash is yin, or darkness... to draw trees or rocks the solid stroke is used; to draw clouds and mists the vacant stroke is used. Through that which is vacant the solid is moved and that which is solid becomes vacant. Thus the entire picture will be full of the life rhythm.[8]

In the use of landscape in painting, the relationship of hills and valleys reveals this rhythm. It is worth looking in passing, if only to hint at the unity of Chinese art with other aspects of daily life, at what Eitel has to say in his book *Feng Shui*, to be looked at in more detail in Chapter 8. In it he says

> ...I have already spoken of those elevations of the ground which

indicate the presence of nature's breath, with its two currents of male and female, positive and negative energy, symbolically called dragon and tiger. The relative position and configuration of these two, the dragon and the tiger, as indicated by hills or mountains, is the most important point, as regards the outlines and forms of the earth's surface. . .

Yin cannot exist without yang. That they are often in imbalance is the root cause of the human tragedy, according to Taoists. Outside the human realm, the whole web of Tao is held together by their interplay. But as Lao Tzu reminds us, they are 'harmonized by the immaterial Breath (ch'i)'. The Pao-p'u tzu states: 'Man exists in ch'i, and ch'i is within man himself. From Heaven and Earth to all kinds of creation, there is nothing which would not require ch'i to stay alive'.

Ch'i fills the internal and external world of the Taoist, vitalizing all things, passing a current of energy to all things animate and inanimate. Taoists believe that it is exhaled in visible form in the mountains as clouds and mist. It is little wonder that clouds and mist, swirling and undulating, figure so largely in their art and poetry and are reflected in their calligraphy and dance. These mystic representations reassure them of the infusion of ch'i in all things, sustaining and invigorating the universe.

Yet he is aware that everything is in a state of flux. A strong wind can change the shape of a cloud, a tumbling river the shape of a river bank, the process of changes in the earth's crust the shape of mountains. Nothing is permanent: everything is the plaything of yin and yang, harmonized by the breath of ch'i yet destined to return to the primordial Tao.

The world of the ten thousand things does not stand still: it is in constant movement, changing, streaming. To fix it, on paper or silk, in stone or clay, or in words, seems on the face of it to be a contradiction.

Yet, somehow, great Chinese artists and poets contrive to convey that streaming, and to maintain those tensions in their audiences, to make the audiences actual participants, and thus to give birth in the next instant to a realization of movement.

The brush, using watery ink on silk or porous paper, assists the painter or calligrapher (very often the same person) in this. Indeed, this medium in particular forces the artist to maintain immediacy. As Watts says, in discussing the art of calligraphy,

If you hesitate, hold the brush too long in one place, or hurry, or try to correct what you have written, the blemishes are all too obvious. But if you write well there is at the same time the sensation that the work is happening on its own, that the brush is writing all by itself — as a river, by following the line of least resistance, makes elegant curves.[9]

There is an immediacy in the execution which is captured on the silk. '. . .there was no second chance. . . Both were subject to the same immediacy as life itself; the movement, the choice was irrevocable, there was no going back and each line had to be in correct relationship with the others.'[10]

It is in the art of calligraphy that the intimate relation of man to the universe is particularly well illustrated. Man is not separated from the rest of creation: he is an integral part of that creation.

The Tao which Taoism knows, and with which its art is concerned, is a seamless web of unbroken movement and change, filled with undulations, waves, patterns of ripples, and temporary 'standing waves' like a river. Every observer is himself an integral function of this web.[11]

'. . .there is at the same time the sensation that the work is happening on its own, that the brush is writing all by itself.'[12]

An illustration that springs to mind is the experience of Eugen Herrigel which he describes so clearly in *Zen in the Art of Archery*:

. . .just as we say in archery that 'It' takes aim and hits. . . What is true of archery and swordsmanship also applies to all the other arts. Thus, mastery in ink-painting is attained only when the hand, exercising perfect control over technique, executes what hovers before the mind's eye at the same moment as the mind begins to form it. . .

We saw in the last chapter that the art of calligraphy was much used in the creation of talismans. The symbolism of yin in fungus, cloud, water and so on, and that of yang in stallion, dragon and the like also played a part in sympathetic magic. Just as calligraphy and graphic art fed into magic, so magic fed into art: the two developed together: both were attempts to control the mysterious and seemingly unpredictable.

Early magic was always of an abstract, non-representational or symbolic, iconic nature. It therefore laid a foundation for abstract art (some of which, coincidentally, bears uncanny resemblance to the work of modern western artists such as Kokoschka [for example, his 'Dents du Midi'] or Youich Inoue ['Drawing']). However, it must be said at once that there the parallel surely ends. Even though Kandinsky, for instance, may say that Western abstract art is the outward expression of an inner urge, it is true to say also that such urges are the by-product of metaphysical anxiety rather than metaphysical certitude.

These Taoist abstractions were, then, graphical representations of such important non-perceptible Taoist concepts as Change, Movement and (importantly from our point of view) Energy. Taoist artists, in making such representations, developed an artistic grammar in which imagination became integrated with actuality. They did this through the portrayal of the most extreme approaches to intangibility accessible to humans, such as mist, clouds, waves, smoke and so on. These nearest representations of the ineffable can be seen in landscape paintings, dance, and even in sculpture and pottery. They thus united what could be seen with what could not be seen: the visible aspects of Energy, Change and Movement with the invisible Ch'i.

This symbolism and abstractionism caught on with all strata of Chinese society from the high-minded to the unsophisticated; abstraction and symbolism can work the imagination of all, at all individual levels.

Legeza makes the interesting point that Ancient China's lack of epic traditions ensured a fertile soil for this abstractionism. There is certainly little doubt that it was popular and began to permeate all other aspects of Chinese art, including dance, poetry, music and drama. In traditional Chinese opera, for instance, the almost bare stage is left to be furnished by the imaginations of the individual members of the audience.

What caught on, and is the most characteristic feature of Taoist art, was the significance of the blank space, of the emptiness or yin which complemented the strength of the yang in a peculiarly telling fashion. This was unsurprising to Taoists, who would have been surprised at any other outcome, but it may help to explain the peculiar fascination which certain strongly Taoist flavoured works of all kinds of art have for Westerners and others outside the mainstream of Chinese thought. There is at least a puzzled recognition of strong forces at play in a work that seems strangely stripped almost bare.

In poetry, too, the same use of space, symbolism and imagery is to be found.

> Mount Lu in misty rain; the river Che at high tide;
> When I had not been there, no rest from the pain of longing.
> I went there and returned... it was nothing special—
> Mount Lu in misty rain; the river Che at high tide.

> The wintry ripples in the lake gently move away;
> White seagulls lightly swoop down.

> There is a meditative terrace left by the ancient Master Chi.
> It is so high that it is always covered by white clouds.
> Should the woodcutter see it, he would not recognize it;
> The mountain monks, however, were glad to find it.
> They thought it would interest me and took
> me there to see it.
> Throughout the night dew drops fall leisurely
> from the bamboos;
> During the day pure breezes blow from the pine grove.
> Meditation is what I used to do as the first thing;
> The terrace of Master Chi inspires me even more.

Or, more briefly,

> Profound quietude delivered me to the transparent moonlight.
> After enlightenment one understands that the 'six Classics'
> contain not even a word.

In these poems there is an economy of words in which each is used with concentrated effect. As in a painting, space is created, and very much is left unsaid, so that the reader or the observer is drawn into actual participation with the artist or poet in achieving the desired end: integration with the Tao.

As in painting, calligraphy, and poetry, so in dance. Here the dancer can be most close to the Tao, in rapt attention to the flow of wu wei, less hindered by any lingering thought of technique, limited only by the limits of the body. Cooper writes,

Dervishes dancing portray the whirling and axial movement of the universe, its folding and unfolding, contraction and expansion, and bring the Supreme Essence into the realm of matter then return it back to the source from which it came. This, also, is perfect yin/yang symbolism, with the Essence as the Tao.[13]

Such dance can be seen in the slow unfolding of T'ai Chi Chuan, in which all outside consciousness is diminished in the meditation in movement which is its essence.

Such meditation in movement is portrayed in all aspects of Taoist and Zen life. Even in the Master instructing a pupil in the art of flower arrangement, this stillness may be seen, as he carefully undoes the ties on the stems, examines each, cautiously bends them to form, and arranges them exquisitely, with no need for any further adjustment, as though he has glimpsed what nature intended.

Thus 'emptiness', or 'no statement', becomes characteristic of all art forms, representing uncertainty, vagueness, and the obscure future which are all characteristic of life in general. The musical pause, the momentary stillness in dance, the meditative pause in instruction, or the enclosed emptiness in painting, calligraphy and poetry: all are inseparable from their opposites. Yin and Yang separately cannot harmonize: they are inseparable, interlocking: without their interlocking harmony, all would be the chaos from which art seeks to escape.

So what of ch'i in all of this? Ch'i is the energy which produces the creative harmony of the yin and the yang, and works for their interlocking. Where does it come from? Modern psychology would say that it is to do with the linking of the right hemisphere of the brain with the left. This is a pleasing, and to Westerners an acceptable, picture of the release of some power not normally available. The Chinese would merely add that the flow of ch'i within the body should not be subject to hindrance if creativity is to be released. When ch'i is flowing freely, as in martial art or the search for immortality, a power that is not normally available is indeed released.

> Ching Hao of the tenth century. . . declares the ch'i is produced 'when the artist's mind does not interfere with the free movement of the brush and thus spontaneously produces the picture without fear.'

In this 'the mind' he refers to is perhaps the left half of it. On the other hand, he certainly does not exclude the necessity for technique, which is a function of the left hemisphere, but sees the need for this only after or in conjunction with using a hat for a brush through the liberation of the right hemisphere.

Although the brush stroke follows certain rules — moves, turns, changes and penetrates — it must not be limited by its quality or form but be as it were flying and flowing.[14]

The painter's total being must be enlisted, as it must be in all exponents of art forms. The ch'i must flow as freely between the hemispheres as it must throughout the body.

6.

Martial Arts

Most philosophies are merely intellectual concepts... Taoist philosophy actually transcends the realm of philosophy because it can be clearly demonstrated through movement in daily life.[1]

Because of his training, an expert martial artist reacts not in a personal way with animosity or ambition, but almost like the operation of a natural law.

For example, I would start to move and my opponent would throw a kick and I would realize that I was moving out of the way of a kick. But I was doing it before I knew why! I just moved, and they would throw a kick and miss![2]

Based on the principle that the human body is a miniature universe, Taoist movement aims to guide an individual's ch'i in a way which exactly follows cosmic law.

There is the story told by Chuang Tzu of an old man who falls into a cataract and comes out downstream quite unharmed. When asked how this came about, he replies, '...Plunging in with the whirl, I came out with the swirl. I accommodate myself to the water, not the water to me. And so I am able to deal with it...'

This exemplifies the use of ch'i through that most subtle principle of Taoism, known as wu wei. Literally, this may be translated as 'not doing', but its proper meaning is to act without forcing — to move in accordance with the flow of nature's course (see also page 118). Perhaps it is best understood from watching the dynamics of water, since we are ourselves eighty per cent water. As the Tao Te Ching has it in chapters 43 and 78, 'The most gentle thing in the world overrides the most hard'; 'Nothing in the world is weaker than water, but it has no better in overcoming the hard'.

The flow of ch'i is the basis of the flowing movements of T'ai
Chi Ch'uan, the 'Taoist dance of the warrior'. All martial arts utilize this principle.

What are the martial arts? There are two categories: they may be
external or internal forms of the art.

External forms are primarily concerned with the bodily skills
used in fighting and self-defence. Karate and Kempo, for example, are thus primarily aimed at developing the body.

Internal forms, on the other hand, aim primarily at self-
understanding and transcendence. Their deepest purpose is not
to impose one's will or cause damage to another, but to serve as
a vehicle of spiritual development, to follow the way of the Tao.
Thus the suffix *do*, meaning way or Tao.

T'ai Chi Chuan and aikido are examples of internal approaches.

Both categories aim at controlling the flow of ch'i, and thus it
is often, not surprisingly, found that practitioners of external practices develop an interest in internal forms.

The Mind: Imagination and Visualization
First the mind, afterwards the body.

The practitioner has to keep his mind on the flow of ch'i, something he can only do through the mind's imagination, through
the meditation in motion which is the basis of martial arts of all
kinds.

What does it mean to do it through the imagination? Since everything we do, from buying a tin of beans to driving a car, is first
done in the mind as a sort of intention pictured in action, then
this is basically to do no more than everyone does every minute
of their life. We all *create* our lives by a process of constantly
imagining, or visualizing, our way through every day. There is nothing strange about visualization. 'You are already using it every day,
every minute in fact. It is your natural power of imagination, the
basic creative energy of the universe which you use constantly,
whether or not you are aware of it.'[3]

The martial artist is aware of it.

The martial arts start with the concentrated mind which the
body thus naturally follows. In the movement of the body there

is meditation. Unlike most forms of meditation, it is meditation in movement.

The mental stillness which is thus achieved in movement is regarded by Taoists in particular as of a higher level than the stillness reached in bodily stillness because it engages the whole psychophysical organism. This has the added advantage that it forms a clear and practical bridge from meditation under the special circumstance of the training hall to meditation under every circumstance of life. A martial artist is able to respond through such practice to each life situation as it comes, unhindered by memories and preconceptions.

The aim is for the mind to move the ch'i calmly and naturally, directing it deeply inward so that it can be gathered into the bones and marrow. The ch'i will then move the entire being smoothly and continuously and the form can easily follow the mind. The spirit is at ease and the body quiet.

At every moment the martial artist must be totally conscious.

No-Mind: *Mushin*
But of what is he totally conscious?

As Takuan said:

> When the swordsman stands against his opponent, he is not to think of the opponent, nor of himself, nor of his enemy's sword movements. He just stands there with his sword which, forgetful of all technique, is ready only to follow the dictates of the unconscious. The man has effaced himself as the wielder of the sword. When he strikes, it is not the man but the sword in the hand of the unconscious that strikes.[4]

Or as a modern master puts it: 'I was able to see what people were going to do before they did it. So in martial arts when someone was going to hit me I would just finish the situation before it got started and that was it.'[5]

Mushin, the doctrine of 'no-mind', indicates that the consciousness must be a detached yet alert consciousness. The mind should not be in any analytical mode, but in a heightened mode of intuitiveness or awareness. The mind has been described as being in a state of 'flowing'. If the flow is interrupted it is injurious. In the case of a fighter it means defeat or even death.

The state of flow referred to is the flow of the ch'i: the martial artist latches on to this flow, and becomes an active part of the universal flux, totally aware of the situation. He experiences oneness with his opponent, and their contest can be likened to a dance.

Breath

As we have seen, the term ch'i is a polymorphous concept, with general connotations of 'breath' being vital energy, vitality, and spirit. In the martial arts, the word for breathing (ch'i) means not only the air that is inhaled and exhaled (coarse ch'i) but also the spirit and intrinsic energy which is centred in the tan t'ien, the psychic centre of the body (subtle ch'i). It is this relation between spiritual breathing and physical breathing that martial artists utilize. Correct use of breathing is valued far more than sheer physical power, for without it, they cannot achieve their goals.

> If the ch'i is dispersed, then it is not stored (accumulated) and is easy to scatter. Let the ch'i penetrate the spine and the inhalation and exhalation be smooth and unimpeded throughout the entire body. The inhalation closes and gathers, the exhalation opens and discharges. Because the inhalation can naturally raise and also uproot the opponent, the exhalation can naturally sink down and also discharge (fa fang) him. This is by means of the i (mind), not the li (strength) mobilizing the ch'i.[6]

The control of the physical breath is important, therefore, to the control of the spiritual breath. Visualizing the passage of the breath helps martial artists to control the circulation of ch'i in their bodies, and, indeed, in directing it towards their partner or opponent.

A Martial Art — T'ai Chi Ch'uan

T'ai Chi Ch'uan is an ancient Chinese exercise derived from Taoist philosophy with roots, it is said, 4000 years old. Based on the Taoist principle that the human body is a miniature universe, Taoist movement aims to guide an individual's ch'i in a way which exactly follows cosmic law. As such it is as good an example of a martial art as any.

T'ai Chi Chuan, like all martial arts, teaches the cultivation of the ch'i within the body and its projection towards one's opponent rather than fighting technique. This emphasizes again that the prerequisite in all forms of martial art is control of the mind, of the breathing and of the flow of ch'i.

Through this concentration on the universal flow of power, this meditation, T'ai Chi Ch'uan enables a person to be calm and self-controlled in everyday life, and to integrate these qualities by means of the external techniques of fighting. Through T'ai Chi Ch'uan, a professional fighter of any discipline or school may learn more about control and balance. And even if a person who practises T'ai Chi Ch'uan has no special training in self-defence, if the occasion should arise in which he (or she) needs to protect himself, he will be spontaneously prepared to do so.

Because of his training, an expert martial artist reacts, as has been said, not in a personal way but like a natural law. He aims to use the most potent of all forces — the power of the Universe itself. It is no real wonder that it is claimed that a force of a thousand pounds can be moved with the movement of a little finger.

T'ai Chi Ch'uan: Practice

Basic requirements for T'ai Chi Ch'uan are concentration, empty-mindedness, relaxation, balance, rhythm, and suppleness.

Concentration
The body always follows the mind.

The aim is for the mind to move the ch'i calmly and naturally, directing it deeply inward for it to be made increasingly subtle and gathered into the bones and marrow. In this way, the ch'i will be available to move the entire being smoothly and continuously; the form easily following the mind. To accomplish this the spine should be erect as if the head were suspended. The mind and ch'i must move flexibly in order to achieve smoothness and roundness of movement.

The abdomen is relaxed, the ch'i is gathered into the bones, the spirit is at ease and the body quiet. At every moment the practitioner must be totally conscious.

To concentrate the energy, the centre of gravity must be lowered, looseness and quietude must be maintained, and the energy focused. The aim of all practice sessions — indeed of everyday life itself — is to use the mind to focus the energy of the subtle ch'i through the use of the coarse ch'i, the breath.

Empty-Mindedness
There is a training exercise called 'Sticking Hands', in which, by touching hands, and following each other's movements, students learn to interpret the silent messages telegraphed by their partner's hands. The way in which a hand retreats can signal a shift of body weight or a change in posture, and in this way a student can become aware of an oncoming attack and react appropriately.

Still and quiet, with the breath sinking to the lower tan t'ien (a spot about two inches below the navel) and remaining there, the martial artist learns to 'listen' to the ch'i as it flows in the total situation existing between himself and his partner.

As a modern Japanese-trained master says,

> When someone hits you, he is extending his ki towards you and it starts to flow when he thinks he will hit you — even before his body moves. His action is directed by his mind. You don't need to deal with his body at all if you can redirect his mind and the flow of his ki[7]

> By paying attention to your ch'i and ignoring your breathing, your striking force will be as strong as pure steel. If you pay attention only to your breathing, your blood circulation will be impeded and your striking force will be inactive and ineffective.

So said Wang Chung Tueh, a T'ai Chi Ch'uan master of the Ming dynasty. By paying attention to the subtle ch'i, he said, and not the coarse, the resulting movements would be like the incessant flow of a great river, with 'all parts of the body connected like a string of pearls'.

Relaxation
In Empty-mindedness there is no room for strain: a natural law does not strain. Even though great energy may be present, there is no straining, no effort.

The martial artist should be in tune with natural law and should exhibit its characteristics. In appearance the martial artist should be like a hawk catching a rabbit. Internally his spirit should be like a cat watching a mouse. 'In resting he should be as still as a mountain; in movement like a river.'

He should store his energy as an archer stores it in a bow, or a hawk in its wings, or a cat in its paw: concentrated and still. In that way he will always have more than he needs and thus be in a position of advantage.

When appropriate, and the flow of ch'i will indicate that moment, he should let the energy go as if releasing an arrow from the energy store of a bow, or from pinions.

His movements should easily follow each other, as they are trained to do in the formalized movements of T'ai Chi Ch'uan, where successive steps follow changes in the form; as they do in a kestrel hovering in air currents, and as they do in a cat stalking its prey: effortless and empty-minded: no sweat.

Balance

There are two rules here.

The first rule is to do with conservation of energy. T'ai Chi Ch'uan is illustrative of this cosmic principle expounded in the Tao Te Ching. In this, Lao Tzu frequently mentions the importance of avoiding fullness. 'Everything in nature follows a cyclical process of growth and evolution . . .' Everything, he says, is subject to birth, growth, maturity, decline, and death before returning to the source of all things, the Tao. It follows then that one should avoid progress beyond a certain point, for decline will inevitably follow fullness.

In movement, then, one never extends one's body or energy completely because this will leave one with no energy in reserve. Instead, one goes only to a certain point, and then draws inward again to the centre to gather one's energy. The movement is repeated, the force is recharged and the energy is recycled at the same time. This is called the law of reversion and clearly depends upon a practical knowledge of yin and yang.

The second rule is to do with standing, with physical immobility. It states that one should stand 'like an unbalanced scale'. This is an essential principle of T'ai Chi Ch'uan. With one's centre of gravity displaced, one can be fluid, ready for action and centrally poised, calm and expanded. So one can protect oneself from all sides. If, on the other hand, a fighter is 'double heavy', that is, with weight evenly distributed on both feet, his ch'i becomes stagnant and he becomes sluggish and incapable of an appropriate response.

Rhythm

Balance implies the use of rhythm, cyclic rhythm. A characteristic of the Universe is, as we have seen, circularity, a succession of cycles. Such rhythm occurs on the microcosmic scale as much as on the macrocosmic.

The body in movement should be like a wheel: in other words it should exhibit cyclical tendencies. 'When a weight comes to my left, my left is empty, and vice versa.' When there is up, there must be down. Yin and yang are given full expression, strength balancing weakness, advance being met by retreat, and retreat by advance.

This is the principle upon which the everyday universe, the ten thousand things, the multi-universe, lives, moves, and has its being through a constant interplay between yin and yang. Yin and yang always complement each other: so they should in movement. 'To stick is to move away, to move away is also to stick.'

The understanding of yin and yang both provides and conserves a practitioner's energy. He finds it is a necessary principle: the polarization it implies, he finds not to be divisive or separating, because it is always integrated by ch'i, the power of the unitary Tao. 'If it were a division . . . the multi-universe would inevitably come to an end.'[8]

In all changing situations, in and out of the training hall, he finds this rhythmic principle of mastery is the same.

Suppleness
There is a good image frequently met with in the literature and the words of masters, to the effect that when one begins to move, the entire body should be like threaded pearls.

The aim must be smoothness, an avoidance of awkwardness. Water is the model: it is never awkward, adapting itself perfectly to all its circumstances. So also should the martial artist. Gaps between movements, any unevenness or discontinuity, are cardinal errors. Feet, legs, and waist should be coordinated so that in moving there is good control of time and space. Without this control the body will be in disorder and the flow of ch'i obstructed.

Suppleness implies continuity. Sudden movement causes the flow of energy to stagnate, for the ch'i is again obstructed, while gentle, rhythmic movement brings about its flowing. Sudden movements also stop suddenly, and cause pauses. As seen above, this inhibits the flow of ch'i and this gives an opponent an advantage because the body is not able to respond fast enough. Without suppleness, the ch'i will be constricted. With light, continuous and flexible movement, on the other hand, the ch'i can be 'expanded with vitality' and the mind remain tranquil.

Ideally, a fly alighting on the arm of a martial artist should be unable to remain because the arm will immediately react to the pressure, and withdraw. Conversely, a fly should be unable to leave an arm, because in attempting to do so, it will release pressure to which the arm will respond by 'sticking' to the fly.

Summary

Martial artists seek to control their ch'i. They use the power of visualization in order to do this. Throughout, their mind is aware of, is visualizing, the movement of the ch'i as it circulates and emerges in the actions of their bodies, the action of their partners' bodies, and, more remotely, in the surrounding situation.

The mind plays its part in the attainment of calmness and tranquillity without which the stored ch'i cannot flow freely. T'ai Chi Ch'uan masters speak of 'the chi as sinking to, and abiding in, the tan t'ien, or circulating throughout the body'. They speak of the mind's mobilizing the ch'i, of the ch'i's mobilizing the body, and of the ch'i being gathered into the bones.

So breath and mind enable the body to respond to external circumstances naturally. At the highest level, masters inquire if the concentration of ch'i has brought the student to the 'pliability of an infant'. This is unlikely to refer merely to the physical characteristics of the martial artist, but will refer also to his mind, which should be without preconceptions, without plans, entirely focused on the total local situation within the larger universe.

> When a person is able to achieve the integration of his own internal polarities through the practice of T'ai Chi Ch'uan, this in turn will cause the response of harmony and unification of all the apparent opposites which appear internally and externally in his life.[9]

T'ai Chi Ch'uan brings the physical, emotional, mental, and spiritual energies into alignment once again as undivided oneness. Note the phrase 'once again'. This is a reference to a return to the infant's pliability, and, beyond that, a return to the state of the uncarved block, that symbol of the primeval Tao from which springs the ten thousand things, which include the small concerns of men.

7.

Health

If you catch one cold in your lifetime then you are physically sick, and if you lose your temper once in a lifetime then you are mentally sick.[1]

This impossible ideal is nevertheless the one that is aimed at in the management of ch'i. It is the ideal of harmony between man and his universe, and between man and his body.

All living things depend for their survival upon a system of homeostasis. The life process is not a series of static conditions: it is a constantly changing series of events occurring as fluctuations between complementary processes. The continued harmony or even existence of the individual, as with the universe itself, depends on the maintenance of his homeostatic yin/yang equilibrium, which depends upon the functioning of the five phases of energy evolution.

In thinking about the interaction of yin and yang, we have seen that Taoists see five interacting phases of energy transformation at play in nature, and therefore also in man.

So the concept of yin/yang and the five types of energy transformation naturally find practical application in Chinese medicine. It serves as an effective means of diagnosis and treatment, and is the basis for the analysis of the functional interactions of the organs.

It is important to remember that the use of the word 'organ' is different in Chinese medicine from that in Western. The Western conception of 'organ' is taken to refer to a physical object to be found in the body. But according to traditional Chinese medicine, the concept of an organ encompasses much more than a mere physical identity. The nearest approach to the Chinese concept is to be found in the Western reference to an organ of the brain: a region of the brain fancied to be concerned with some mental or moral quality. So in China an organ is defined by role: each 'organ' having a specific role in the processing, storage, and distribution of ch'i. There is thus a mental and spiritual aspect to the word. Such an organ may or may not have a physical counterpart. An example of a Chinese organ without a physical counterpart is the 'triple burner'.

Taoist healing deals with twelve such 'functional energy spheres', which are: lung, large intestine, stomach, spleen/pancreas, heart, small intestine, bladder, kidney, circulation, triple burners, gall bladder, and liver.

Ancient Taoists saw that illness often produced painful areas on skin which disappeared when a cure was effected. They saw also that sedation or stimulation of various points on the body affected the functioning of internal organs. After many years of observation of treatment and response, the distribution of such points — four hundred on the head alone — was effected, and, by joining the points, meridian paths were mapped. These traced the flow of ch'i as it circulated. Since ch'i was a cosmic force, they reasoned that the meridian pathways connected not only the organs to one another but each of them to the cosmos.

The study and use of these internal and external pathways is what Taoist medicine is all about.

Table 2:

Name of meridian	Yin/Yang	Element	Peak hours
lung	yin,	metal,	0300-0500
large intestine,	yang,	metal,	0500-0700
stomach,	yang,	earth,	0700-0900
spleen/pancreas,	yin,	earth,	0900-1100
heart,	yin,	fire,	1100-1300
small intestine,	yang,	fire,	1300-1500
bladder,	yang,	water,	1500-1700
kidney,	yin,	water,	1700-1900
circulation/sex	yin,	fire,	1900-2100
triple burners,	yang,	fire,	2100-2300
gall bladder,	yang,	wood,	2300-0100
liver,	yin,	wood,	0100-0300

There are twelve such meridians, and they are seen in Table 2. Their relationship to the five elements is illustrated, and the time of day when treatment is best effected according to the Chinese two-hour system is also shown.

There are eight other meridians important to Taoism: (1) *Tu Mai*, corresponding to the spinal cord; (2) *Jen Mai*, corresponding to the central nervous system and the visceral organs; (3) *Tai Mai* to the kidneys; (4) *Yang wei* and (5) *Yin wei* have a close correspondence to the brain; (6) *Yang Ch'iao* and (7) *Yin Ch'iao* are related to the genital nervous system including the prostate gland and the nerve functions in the hands and feet, and (8) *Chong Mai* starts in men between the testes and the penis and in women similarly, and passes up through the stomach and heart and thence to the centre of the head. Some of these organs will be met with again when we come to consider the question of immortality.

The ch'i flows through the twelve meridians constantly, and on its unimpeded flow depends the health of the body. Every facet of our being is a manifestation of energy. It is the vital energy or ch'i which enables blood to circulate, glands to secrete, breathing, excretion, every bodily activity, and all metabolic processes to take place. As Ni, Hua Ching says,

> The presence or absence of the heartbeat is the indication used to determine whether a person is alive or dead, but what is it that determines whether the heart beats or ceases to beat? The heart beats because the vital energy (yuan ch'i) dwells within the body. If the vital energy leaves us, the body becomes like a dry, empty shell devoid of all life. So it is not our outer form upon which our lives depend, but rather it is the subtle ch'i upon which our outer, physical form depends.[2]

When the energy flows through the meridians unimpeded and the various organs are in a state of equilibrium, one is healthy.

Conversely, according to ancient Chinese medical theory, disease is the manifestation of energy disorder and aberration within the body. It is a state in which the various organs and the nervous system are functioning incorrectly or inadequately in a manner which is either too slow or too fast, or too weak or too strong. If the ch'i becomes imbalanced or blocked, disease manifests.

Disease occurs when the mind and body are out of harmony. The activity of the mind in directing ch'i is fundamental. Its use or non-use must directly affect the dynamic processes taking place along the meridians, and this in turn must affect the physical. The flow of energy in the body is influenced not only by one's conscious thoughts but by the emotions one experiences. If one particular emotion or mode of thinking is habitually emphasized, a particular organ may become over-stimulated, causing depletion, imbalance and blockage within the meridian system.

The energy flow may also be influenced for ill by the fact that too often mental activity is quite unrelated to physical activity. It is in their encouragement of 'present-moment thinking' that disciplines such as T'ai Chi Ch'uan are valuable.

In any case, whatever the cause, disease indicates that the energy flow needs to be corrected. The essential art of traditional Chinese medicine presents three aspects: to foresee, to prevent, and to cure.

As regards foreseeing, this is achieved through the observation of the flow of ch'i and may be done through the use of the pulse. To take the pulse, a Taoist doctor uses three fingers. With these three fingers he is able to observe six pulses on each wrist, a total of twelve, one for each of the meridians.

By feeling these twelve pulses, it is possible for him to understand the state of ch'i in each, and to have advance warning of disease, for he will immediately notice any irregularities.

Table 3:

Left radial artery	*Light pressure*	*Deep pressure*
Index finger	Small intestine	Heart
Middle finger	Gall bladder	Liver
Third finger	Urinary bladder	Kidneys
Right radial artery		
Index finger	Large intestine	Lungs
Middle finger	Stomach	Spleen
Third finger	Triple Burner	Heart Controller

For the prevention of disease, the internal ch'i needs to be mobilized, after a thorough examination through the pulse, and by the usual observation and questioning of the patient.

> What is motionless is easy to hold;
> What is not yet foreshadowed is easy
> to form plans for;
> What is fragile is easy to break;
> What is minute is easy to disperse.
> Deal with a thing before it comes into existence;
> Regulate a thing before it gets into confusion.

The common people in their business often
fail on the verge of succeeding
Take care with the end as you do with the beginning,
And you will have no failure.[3]

For the cure of disease through the mobilization of ch'i, it is again the pathways of ch'i that are used. These pathways cannot be acted on directly. The only points at which the ch'i flow may be effectively and predictably controlled are those points mapped so painstakingly so long ago. They are known as acupuncture points, because the chief traditional means of influence is by inserting and manipulating a needle.

These may be mobilized by needle, pressure, massage, or heat treatment — though not all the points are to be used in the latter. Whatever method is used, the aims are the same, namely, to stimulate or to sedate: to encourage the flow of ch'i, or to slow it.

Acupuncture (*hsa chien pen*) is a very precise science or technology. Its practice is based upon the principle, seen above in Table 2, that ch'i is flowing through a specific channel during each double hour and that in each double hour, therefore, a particular organ is ripe for attention.

The skill of the practitioner is not only in the manipulation of the needle, but also in knowing the type of needle to be used, as well as in the diagnosis of the disease.

Acupuncture, a cold, yin, treatment, is largely used for correcting yang excesses and the relief of pain. It has been shown that for the relief of pain at least, acupuncture is successful in 93% of cases.[4].

Acupressure (*tien chen*) operates on the acupuncture points without the use of needles. In it the practitioner uses the tip of thumb or forefinger, the nail of either, or the knuckle of the second finger. He may also use a blunt needle, rather like the rubber tip to a pencil. The aims of acupressure are the same as in acupuncture. The means, however, seem less precise.

The same could be said of massage. Again, Taoist massage technique (*amno*) makes use of knowledge of meridians and pressure points in order to energize or sedate the flow of ch'i. As always, a deep background knowledge of methods of diagnosis is also needed.

Finally, direct action on the acupuncture points may be attempted by means of heat treatment (*Wen Chiech'u*). This form of treatment is mainly used to cope with excesses of cold yin.

It is done through the burning of the mugwort plant (*Artemisia vulgaris*).

At one time, and not so long ago, the burning took place directly on the surface of the skin; nowadays, the leaves are burnt in a container which is then held close to the chosen acupuncture point. The heat activates the ch'i to flow.

Heat treatment is often used in conjunction with acupuncture in order to fine-tune the flow of ch'i.

A further treatment by doctors is noteworthy. It is the use of magical talismans, which has been discussed in Chapter 4. Such methods have no doubt become less common, but it may be that their turn will come again, if only because of the increasing attention being paid to the use of placebos in Western medicine.

The treatment of a sick person by talisman is described in full in Legeza's *Tao Magic* and briefly goes as follows:

The patient tells the Taoist doctor his symptoms, and is led to the image of the Yellow Emperor and bows four times. The doctor recites seven incantations to do with the making of the talisman: water, cinnabar, ink, brush, paper, writing the selected charm, and finally summoning the spirits of the appropriate branch of medicine. Then the doctor paints the charm, silently repeating the Yellow Emperor's chant for healing. When finished, he writes 'chih ling' (meaning 'induced to come') at the top of the paper. He sprinkles three drops of water on the 'summoning the spirits' charm, takes a mouthful of water and sprays it over the talisman he has just created. Then he makes the healing spirit incantation, clicks his teeth three times to denote a pause, bows, picks up the talisman and retires. Finally, he wraps the talisman in white paper and gives it to the patient with instructions on how to burn it (to send it to the spirits) and what additional drugs to take. The patient must take the talisman home in his left hand.[5].

Magic or science? That is a question which the Western mind must find difficult to resist, not only in respect of magical charms, but in respect of the whole concept of ch'i meridian pathways in the body.

So much, then, for the control of ch'i by the doctor. We can now turn to do-it-yourself methods: self-massage, breathing, and diet.

Do-it-yourself methods do not necessarily involve or require knowledge of acupuncture points or meridian pathways, though it must increase their effectiveness if these are known. The use of the mind in imagining the flow of ch'i certainly increases their effectiveness.

This is so in self-massage.

In breathing exercises, too, Wang Yung Chueh says, 'Let the mind direct the ch'i so that it sinks deeply and steadily and can permeate the bones. Let the ch'i circulate throughout the entire body freely and without hindrance so that the body will follow the dictates of the mind'.

It is not just a matter of physical technique: it involves mental activity as well.

There are forty distinct methods of breathing recognized by Taoists. All are based on yin and yang and the rules of the five elements. Some of them facilitate the flow of ch'i, some block it, while some are set to cultivate the internal ch'i for use in martial arts, for instance.

> In the exercise, one needs to imagine or visualize that there is such ch'i . . . in the body that can be directed to go in regular lines. In the long run, through long visualization, meditation, contemplation, as well as auto-suggestion, the extension of control over the central nervous system is possible.[6]

The long-term objective of those who practice Taoist breathing, to be examined in more detail in Chapter 10 is to reach the stage of breathing without either inhaling or exhaling: to practice what Chuang Tzu, among others, described as breathing through the heels. It is not immediately clear what is valuable about this achievement. As Chee Soo says, 'Only students who have spent many years practising. . . will fully appreciate what this means and how it is accomplished'.[7]

At an everyday mundane level, breathing exercises are used to direct the ch'i in ways that clear the head, renew sexual potency, heal wounds, as well as cure diseases.

As regards diet, we move away from expressly working on the ch'i and its pathways and are more in the field of using food to clear the grosser pathways affected by ch'i.

How does diet help to maintain or regain good health? First, it helps to ensure that the organs of the body are able to work at 100 per cent efficiency: to do this it is necessary to get rid of surplus fat, excess water, toxins, and acidity that accumulate. Second, it ensures that the digestive system is working efficiently, so that food consumed is digested well and circulated quickly.

Elimination is affected by food: it is well known, for instance, that the elimination of meat takes days, compared to the hours taken by vegetable food. For good health, waste products should be eliminated without delay. Third, the blood and all body fluids should be of the right composition and should circulate easily.

To achieve this involves eating only natural foods: those not tainted by pesticides, fertilizers, bleaches, additives, colourings, preservatives, and flavourings.

A strict Taoist diet (*Ch'ang Ming*) is strict indeed. Foods that are never to be eaten include processed grain foods, deep fried food, coffee, alcohol, tobacco, chocolate and other sweets, spices, rock salt, mustard, pepper, vinegar, pickles, curry, red meats, salmon, tuna, mackerel, shark, swordfish or whale, sugar, ice cream, jellies, synthetic fruit juices, potatoes, tomatoes, aubergines, rhubarb, spinach, meat extracts, soups or gravies, cheese, milk, butter, boiled or fried eggs, lard or dripping from animals, and any fat birds or fish.

It is claimed that strictly following this regime for three years will result in the creation of new skin tissue throughout the organs, flesh and muscles. By ten years it is claimed that there will be a renewal of all nails, teeth and bones.[8]

A less strict regime is one that returns to a consideration of the Five Elements. In this, foods that are related to the organs as symbolic of the Elements are recommended. For instance, sour foods are recommended for the liver, hot foods for the lungs, and so on. An ideal daily diet contains all five varieties of food: sour, bitter, sweet, hot, and salty, with more or less of each according to the needs of the individual. Foods which are prone to cause an imbalance in the system are much fat, cold and raw foods, much liquid, and very dry or excessively bitter food.[9].

Magic or science?

The definition of science is, as we have seen, 'knowledge ascertained by observation and experiment, critically tested, systematized and brought under general principles...'. The Chinese would claim, with justification, that their study of those intangible pathways of ch'i as means of achieving internal and external harmony satisfies such criteria, certainly on the operating table, in the doctor's surgery, in breathing exercises, and in diet.

Whether the same criteria are satisfied in the use of talismans to achieve similar effects is a question to which the answer may be found as part of 'the proof of the pudding'.

8.

Feng Shui

If a geomancer can recognize ch'i, that is all there is to feng shui.[1]

To the Taoists, man, living creatures, the earth, and the cosmos
have always comprised one 'living, breathing organism' through
which ch'i flows and pulses. The art of Feng Shui, literally wind
and water, is concerned with those currents as they flow through
the earth and as their results affect the fate of man. Its aim is to
detect and facilitate the flow of the earth's ch'i just as the goal of
acupuncture is to tap the flow of bodily ch'i in a beneficent manner.
Chinese geomancy ('divination by figures of or on earth') uses
an understanding of ch'i more than anything else. Detecting and
channelling the forces of ch'i has necessitated an intense interest
in the lie of the land, in astronomy, astrology, time, meteorology,
and mythology. It is by no means a lost art, but still plays an important part in architecture and town planning, in interior design
and landscape gardening.

Everything: hills, streams, trees, stones, and humans, inhale and
exhale ch'i, thus affecting each other. Ch'i changes and pulses
within the earth according to cosmic tides, which are detectable
and controllable. As Sarah Rosbach says in her book, based largely
on the contact she had with a Black Hat Feng Shui *hsien sheng*,

> In the course of its turning, ch'i may rise near to the earth's surface,
> creating mountains. It may expand so strongly as finally to escape,
> erupting into a volcano. And if ch'i recedes too far from the earth's
> crust, the land will be dry, desert-like and flat. The best situation
> occurs when ch'i nearly brushes the earth's surface, causing moun-
> tains to form, trees to grow tall, grass to be green, air to be fresh,
> water to be clear, clean and accessible, flowers to bloom, and man

to live comfortably and contentedly. Where ch'i is too far away, no water flows, pollution and sickness thrive, and there will be bad luck.[2]

The mapping of the pathways of ch'i within the human body, difficult though it is, is simple when compared to the difficulties encountered when trying to do the same with the currents within the earth. Man is certainly too small in comparison to the earth to be able to see the master map, and even experiences great difficulty in local mapping. It is as if he was reduced in size to that of a single atom, and was set to try to detect the flow of ch'i within one whorl of his middle finger's print. Ch'i exists, and powerfully so, but is subject to the great flows around it of which he has only a faint inkling except when they affect his fate.

Nevertheless, the flow is detectable and controllable. The Taoist believes that he can detect the flow of ch'i by examining the land-scape around him and by examining the larger currents that guide the stars in their courses. He believes that currents of ch'i are detectable in the landscape: that the forces and nature of the invisible ch'i currents, known also as 'dragon's veins', are determined not only by mountains and hills (yang), and valleys and water-courses (yin), but also by the movements of the heavenly bodies from hour to hour and day to day. It is as if the local characteristics of the finger whorl indicate the presence of ch'i by bumps and indentations, and as if the atom sized feng shui practitioner is aware not only of the mighty body around him, with its perio-dicities, but of the cosmic environment beyond even that, also subject to flows and pulses of ch'i, all of which affect his finger whorl.

On earth, he has detected such a periodicity: he believes there is a change in the quality of ch'i every two hours which will not be repeated for sixty years: the quality of the ch'i at any particu-lar time will affect an enterprise commenced at that time for sixty years at least, so that the time of commencement of an enter-prise is a matter of much importance, subtlety, and anxiety. Any enterprise of moment, such as building, altering, moving, buying or selling property which can be affected by the state of ch'i neces-sitates a good knowledge of the clock and the calendar, since both are involved in the flow of that ch'i.

Geomancy, then, is concerned with the art of determining the position of the sites of houses for the living and tombs for the dead so that they are in harmony with the local currents of ch'i.

If houses and tombs are not correctly sited, evil effects will befall
the inhabitants of the houses and the descendants of the dead,
whereas a good siting will bring them happiness, prosperity, and
longevity.

A site will have an 'optimum gateway to good fortune' determined by ch'i, clock and calendar, which may not be at a con-
venient time. Consequently, building of houses may be delayed
for a very long time. Likewise burials: the bones may be kept in
store in pots on hillsides (and the pots and contents were known
by Christian missionaries, if Stephen Skinner is to be believed,
as 'potted chinamen').

It is unlikely that the channels of ch'i that are detected by feng
shui methods have any direct counterparts in western science.
But, as with acupuncture, the proof is in the result. Certainly, vast
numbers of Chinese have throughout the ages relied on the skills
of their feng shui hsien sheng to protect themselves and their
kin from danger, and to increase their good fortune. Today, too,
sophisticated Chinese who make full use of Western technology
still make sure that feng shui indications are favourable to them
before undertaking new projects, or burying their parents. Somewhere in them, not far beneath the Western veneer, are racial
memories of dragons and tigers, no more strange than the sub-
conscious of the western city gent avoiding walking beneath a
ladder.

Dragons figure largely in Chinese thought. Feng shui recognizes
not only ch'i but ascribes to the earth animal, human, and mytho-
logical characteristics.

The dragon, for instance, gives prosperity, and is the symbol
of all social, moral, or political exaltation. In feng shui, they are
believed to be the carriers of ch'i, and for feng shui purposes may
be either water dragons or mountain formation dragons.

Water dragons are best detected in meandering streams and the
sky. If the course of a river is a meandering one, that is sure evidence of the presence of a dragon: he prefers curves to crooked
paths. They are highly revered and feared by the Chinese, for they
are the source of fertility, and of floods. They are revered for the
quality of their strength and power: the strength of water so
beloved of Lao Tzu and Chuang Tzu: strength in weakness, fluidity,
adaptability, coolness of judgement, restraint, gentle persuasion,
and passionlessness. At the same time, water, in uncontrolled angry
flood and torrent is anything but gentle, so they are to be feared
as well. So much so that in early days, water dragons were

propitiated by the sacrifice of young girls in the rivers to be their brides.

As they move through the air, their forms are adopted by the clouds. So the superior power of water dragons is seen also in the fact that the very shape of mountain formation dragons is conditioned by the flight and return of the water dragons, or, as we would say, the earth is shaped by the water cycle they represent.

In addition, water, in the feng shui system, is always looked on as symbolic of wealth and affluence. If water runs off in a straight line, so too do the money and riches of people living in the vicinity.

Water courses, indeed, are the most obvious flow lines of ch'i. If fast flowing water, or straight flowing water, rapidly conducts ch'i away, slow sinuous courses accumulate ch'i, especially if they form a pool. Water, if curved and well placed, will contain the ch'i.

Thus, feng shui hsien sheng are much concerned with the state of the water courses and pools in the vicinity of a site under consideration. They are also much concerned with mountain formation dragons, with the evidence of the flow of ch'i to be seen in the landscape. In what appear now to be figurative terms, they looked for evidence in the hills and mountains of a dragon shape and for evidence of his mating with his opposite number in heaven, the white tiger.

The yin and yang currents were identified with the Tiger and the Dragon, which in turn represented the western and eastern quarters of heaven. The east heaven is ruled by the azure dragon, the west by the white tiger. Ranges of hills which conformed in their conjunction to this visual pattern of a mating of dragon and tiger were much sought after as propitious sites for graves or houses.

> The image is clear: the greatest generation of ch'i occurs at the point where the loins of the dragon and the tiger are locked together in intercourse. The sexual nature of the spot where there is some 'sudden transition from male to female' is the link between ch'i as applied to the body of the earth and ch'i as applied to the body of man: in each case it is the same force which is generated by sexual intercourse.[3]

If the classic dragon/tiger situation is not apparent, then at least completely flat ground should be avoided or mounds or trees placed. Boldly rising elevations are yang, softly undulating ground is yin. Where yang predominates, the site should be at a place where yin characteristics are found by sight or compass in some significant degree. Predominantly female ground looks for conjunction (copulation) with yang ground. In any case it should be a spot where there is transition from male to female, male predominating if possible. The classic proportions are three-fifths yang to two-fifths yin.

Mountains were particularly potent, not only as traditionally clear evidence of dragons and for being the abode of immortals, but because of their association with planets. Which one they are associated with is found by an examination of their summits — for example, a high mountain with a softly rounded peak is the representation of Venus, and according to the theory of the Five Elements, the element of metal rules. The client's birth date is therefore important in the selection of a site overlooked by hills and mountains. 'Thus a person born in the dragon month will be at home with fire hill, but a person born in a wood month would encounter disaster if he was buried within sight of such a hill: the symbolic possibility of a conflagration is obvious.'[4]

Just as in the body, so in the earth, there is the possibility of things going wrong: Chinese medicine is as much or more to do with prevention as with cure. So the hsien sheng made it their business to detect bad influences as well as good in order to counteract any harmful effects.

Eitel speaks of a 'poisonous deadly exhalation of nature's breath,' (sha ch'i). In general, the existence of such a breath will be betrayed by a hill or mountain running sheer up in bold straight lines, or looking exceedingly rough and rugged without any gradual slopings. All straight lines — known as 'secret arrows' — are to be avoided, most especially when a straight line points towards the chosen site. Or if a ridge of railway embankment runs across the frontage in a straight line, then that, too, is most inauspicious. Detached rocks and boulders are also malign, unless they are screened by trees and bushes.

It is in their positive avoidance of straight lines that the Chinese very often differ from the West. Where straight lines are unavoidable, as in the building of houses or cities, then great care and ingenuity is taken to block off these 'secret arrows' by means of screens.

Two thousand years ago, the Chinese became aware that the earth's magnetic force affected living creatures. It was only in the 1970s that Western scientists also discovered this when they found that certain bacteria appeared to be organic magnets in that they swam towards the north or south depending on the hemisphere they were found in.

This ancient discovery turned the minds of Chinese feng shui hsien sheng towards the possibility that there might be a connection with the flow of ch'i. It was this that started the development of the formidable feng shui compass, the *lo p'an,* used to refine their visual observation of water courses and mountains.

This instrument, several inches across, has a compass needle at its centre, and this is surrounded by up to thirty-eight concentric rings, from the innermost with the eight trigrams of the I Ching inscribed, to the outer on which is inscribed the Chinese zodiac. In between, there are conventional compass points, compass points offset by small amounts, rings which allow for reference to astrology, to the sixty year calendar, and degrees indicating days of the year, and so on. This highly complicated and refined instrument is used by most feng shui hsien sheng in order to take bearings on and thus ascertain the relative importance of dragon veins and other features as they interact with one another,

> Thus the direction of the dragon veins, especially where they come to a head, which may be a cliff or the end of a line of hills, the position of pools or lines of drainage, levees, intersection of rivers (even paths, railway tracks and existing architectural lines) must be taken into account, as each may carry some part of the flow of ch'i through the landscape.[5]

It is clear that the choice of a site must more often than not be dictated by a careful balancing of benign and malign influences: only the most fortunate (or the most wealthy or powerful) can nowadays hope for a site completely free of bad influences. In the past it was difficult enough: not only were the topographical features to be taken into consideration, but more intangible influences had to be considered, such as birth sign, position in family, and so on. Nowadays, the effects of overpopulation and consequent crowding of competing interests increase the difficulties of feng shui hsien sheng.

Much of feng shui is to do with the best siting for the family grave, but it aims equally to ensure that the living are cared for and protected from harm. The use of the lo p'an allows the feng shui hsien sheng to indicate which six consecutive days of the year are propitious not only for burials, but to the commencement of work on any site.

Large Chinese banks and business houses ensure that they have a feng shui reading to hand when new plans are in the making, so it is understandable that the Chinese businessman looks to the same art to ensure safety and good fortune at home.

A house or a room is like a body, having its own metabolism. Its occupants are its organs, to be nourished by a healthy and balanced flow of ch'i. Traditional houses, including those built in towns and cities, were built around a central court: it was believed that, no matter how far from the country, the residents should never lose touch with the elemental universe. So they kept Nature just outside in the central courtyard, where there would be rocks, bonsai and water. The garden was seen as a reflection of the macrocosm, so that every opportunity was taken to encourage the interplay of yin and yang. Mountains, valleys, rivers and lakes were all represented. Flowing water and still water symbolized movement and repose, the complementary opposites, and water-worn stones symbolized the interaction of the soft and the hard.

It was probably not accidental that there was much use of water, the home of the water dragon and the symbol of wealth and affluence.

Around the garden the rooms faced inward, turning the inhabitants away from the working world towards the ideal of simple nature.

It follows that considerable ingenuity is necessary to provide the same sort of ch'i-positive nature-aware environment now that more and more people live in overcrowded cities, where 'secret arrows' are, as it were, built into the environment. So it is not surprising that hsien sheng command large fees.

If possible, access to a house should not be direct because of these 'secret arrows'. For this reason, in rural south China, all villages and isolated houses have a little grove of trees behind them and at the very least have a pond in front. This keeps away the bad breath of inauspicious ch'i. In towns and cities, particularly modern ones, only the richest can afford the space or money to provide a remedy such as even a small pond to deflect such malign ch'i.

At the very least, drives should not be straight, nor homes situated at the end of a long straight street. Stories abound of misfortune descending on people foolish enough to ignore such obvious omens, and whose good luck only recovered after remedial steps had been taken.

So, though it is necessary to allow the entry of beneficient ch'i, it is equally necessary to prevent the ingress of sha ch'i. Fortunately the two differ in an important respect: sha ch'i is confined to straight lines, while ch'i moves in dragon-like curves and spirals. So, although windows and doors need to be open to the ingress of ch'i, they can be protected from 'secret arrows' by means of screens and complicated entrances. If the family cannot afford these, then written plaques or reflecting mirrors can be placed to defend their doorways.

Inside the house, every effort should be made to ensure that the ch'i is allowed to circulate. The essence of good feng shui is to accumulate ch'i without allowing it to go stagnant: for instance, a bedroom should not be placed over an empty room or garage, because stagnant ch'i will accumulate there and infect the room above.

The placing of furniture should not obstruct the circular flow of ch'i from room to room; similarly, the doors and windows should encourage this circular flow. It should be easy to move from room to room without bumping into corners or furniture: ch'i has been compared to a dancer who cannot perform well on a cluttered stage.

In urban areas, it seems that mirrors are essential. These can be used to reflect bad ch'i away, back to its source. Someone has called mirrors 'the aspirin of Feng Shui.' In ancient days, they were worn on the breast or shield, and acted as amulets. Nowadays, hung inside and outside houses, they perform the same sort of function. They may be used to provide doors where none exist, or to widen rooms to provide better proportions. The most popular kind of mirror is the *Pa gua* which is a small round mirror having a wooden frame with the I Ching trigrams on it.

All this is merely carrying on what the feng shui proponents have always recommended. As Eitel wrote, 'Heaven, it is said, requires the aid of man to carry out its scheme of justice. Earth requires the aid of man to bring its products to absolute perfection'. Man's place in all things is to carry out the will of heaven by maintaining the balance and harmony between the yin and yang. He does this in his environment through feng shui by means of landscape architecture, town planning, and careful planning of the interior of his home.

All forms of Taoist-inspired art and science are aimed at being the outward and visible expression of ch'i. All creation should be in yin/yang accord, whether it be in painting, poetry, music, the creation of a garden, a landscape or a townscape.

The natural home of men and women should be where feng shui influences create harmony with ch'i. An ideal site 'is one protected from high winds by a northern screen of hills or trees, a place in which streams and rivers meander slowly, and which nestles in the embrace of hills rather like an armchair, with a view preferably to the south.'

It is worth saying at this point that it is very odd that so much attention is paid to water (shui) in the science of feng shui, and so very little paid to wind (feng).

Wind seems to be avoided whenever possible. Ch'i is said to ride on the wind and disperse, so if the site is windblown from every direction, then the ch'i will be scattered before it can accumulate. Ch'i can be encouraged to gather by mellow winds, but who can trust the wind to remain mellow? On the whole, it seems best to keep out of the wind and, if this is not possible, to screen and protect the site whenever possible by means of tree wind-breaks.

Nevertheless, it must be remembered that the wind performs two important functions. First, it carries the dragons of water aloft to form clouds and rain and continue the cycle that refreshes and invigorates the earth. Related to this is the fact that wind is, together with water, one of the weather ch'i which are said to mediate between Heaven and Earth. In modern parlance, feng and shui together may be said to form active constituents in the mantle of atmosphere which protects us from the naked power of the sun and space.

> Only in places where the breath of nature is well kept together, being shut in to the right and left and having a drainage carrying off the water in a winding tortuous course, there are the best indications of a permanent supply of vital breath being found there.[6]

Such ideals were always difficult to attain, and remain so in rural areas. What is interesting is to see how the old skills of the feng shui hsien sheng are still being used and adapted to today's vastly more complex urban landscape.

9.

Immortality: The Elixir of Life

In Taoist temples incense burning is a central rite. The curling smoke suggests ch'i and the principle of change that permeates the universe, and the scent evokes thoughts suitable to the setting, becoming a 'perfume that deifies'. The temple attendants who look after the incense burners and the altar are known as 'furnace masters'; in this can be seen ancient alchemical connections. Alchemists have always been known for their skill in making incense and perfumes, and incense has always, throughout the world, been employed in purification and as a homage to divinities.

This chapter deals with alchemy as practised throughout the world, and particularly with Chinese practices. Universally, the main objects of alchemy appear in the popular mind to have numbered two. The first was the transmutation of base metal into gold, and the second the search for the Philosopher's Stone, the elixir of life, supposed to confer immortality. This potion was sometimes imagined as a powder, sometimes as a fluid. With the Chinese preoccupation with immortality, a preoccupation not shared with other cultures, it is not surprising that they tended to concentrate more on that aspect than the former. Nevertheless, the true object of the secret methods was often concealed under the cloak of a search for gold, as commonly happened elsewhere.

Indeed, secrecy has always surrounded the subject like a cloak, in order that the high arts were not revealed to persons unfitted or unready to partake of them. It makes the task of investigating the ancient art very difficult for one who is not an adept.

One form of alchemy, in which immortality was sought through sexual practices, is unique to Taoism and will therefore be looked at in detail in the next chapter. Basic to this, as to all alchemy, was the concept of transmutation: in its case, the transmutation of *ching*, seen as sexual fluid, into ch'i, and thence to pure spirit.

While, in both East and West, alchemy was practised or patronized by people hoping for riches, power or immortality, such a patronage could have disastrous results for those failing to deliver the goods. It is not surprising that all alchemists without exception warned against getting involved with princes and other patrons.

Peculiar to Taoism is the non-belief in an afterlife, coupled with a consequent deep concern with immortality. While certain alchemists and their patrons were no doubt concerned with getting rich quick, the main concern of Taoists has always been to live long in order to have time in which to learn to fly the clouds one day with the gods.

Joseph Needham suggests that Chinese alchemy has three roots. The first is concerned with the search for herbs and other plants that can confer long life; the second with practices for transmuting metals into gold; and the third with the making and use of potions for health and immortality.[1]

He does not apparently consider that these three roots include practices to do with spirituality. In this he may be mistaken: a search for immortality may well have had spiritual overtones.

China has a rich history of using herbs and other plants as a basis of good and life-long health. Even today, certain regimens are stated to allow long life, ages of 150 or 200 years being claimed. Quite simply, the health of the human body is seen to be based on a form of ch'i known as *Neichung Ch'i* which can be strengthened by all forms of Taoist yoga, and especially by strict adherence to the sort of regime mentioned in Chapter Seven, together with yogic breathing exercises. Correctly following this 'Way of Occlusion' (*Ch'ili Nung*) will lead to strength of muscles, suppleness of tendons and sinews, and lead to the bones becoming hard, resilient, and supple, a result, as we shall see, similar to that attained through sexual alchemy.[2] The secret of immortality itself may not have been discovered by taking this non-alchemical route, but definite claims for longevity are made. In China in particular, whose people had never been over enthusiastic about the idea of reincarnation, any route to extended life as a means of attaining wisdom and fulfilment was to be regarded favourably.

The second and third of Needham's categories of Chinese alchemy are perhaps best summed up by John Blofeld. He mentions the *Ts'an T'ung Ch'i* (roughly translated as 'The Union Of Three'), which, as he says, appears to be a treatise on a number of objectives of alchemy. On the face of it this seems to describe a method of transmuting base metals into gold. In addition he says it appears to be describing a method of making a golden pill or potion of perennial youth, longevity, or immortality; a way to create by sexual or non-sexual means a spirit body capable of enjoying eternal life, and finally to provide a means whereby one becomes pure spirit.[3]

As with sexual alchemy, the base metal (equivalent to ching, sexual fluid), was to be transmuted into ch'i, and this in turn transmuted into gold (the refined metal equivalent to pure spirit). This is the union of three. The close parallel between the two methods reflected the Taoist belief that identical laws are everywhere apparent — and that ch'i is manifest everywhere.

It is by now generally accepted that alchemy did not in fact refer merely to changing the chemical constituents of matter, but more importantly to changing the spiritual being of the alchemist. (*Urum nostrum non est aurum vulgum*: our gold is not the common gold.) The transmutation of baser metals into gold may or may not have been possible, but the process is more often understood to be a symbol for the transmutation of some of the psycho-physical elements of humans from an impure, obstructed state to a pure, open state of responsiveness to finely tuned energy. In China, this was the ch'i. Similarly the Hindu praṅa, Greek pneuma, Jewish ruah, Western ideas of vital force, *élan vital*, spirit, ether: all these can be equated with ch'i as representative of the vital breath of the universe, which through the manifestation of agents of change (in the Chinese cosomology, the yin and the yang) could be used by alchemists in their efforts at producing change.

Note the use above of the word psycho-physical: it is not, has not ever been, merely a matter of spiritual progress isolated from the body: it has been recognized, perhaps nowhere so clearly as in Taoism, that there can be no spiritual progress without an effect upon the physical being of the seeker. We see it claimed that the very constitution of the bones is changed in the successful seeker after immortality. Taoists will say that since everything in the cosmos consists of energy in various states from gross to subtle, and since all of the cosmos is affected by all of its aspects, it would be strange indeed if a growing spiritual sensitivity to subtler forms of energy was not paralleled by similar changes in the physical body. Just as precious metals were regarded as the most evolved forms of the minerals, so, by analogy, to 'make gold by our art' was to make oneself into a more highly evolved member of the human race.

It is possible that alchemists were seekers after human spiritual evolution first and students of chemical science second; except that the two were closer in Taoist alchemy than in others. All had as their goal the evolutionary transformation of man's total being. They believed that he was a microcosm, that the processes they observed and studied externally in nature could also be observed and studied internally.

That fire and cauldrons were used by alchemists of all persuasions is not to be denied. Many were seeking base-metal transmutation if only as an experimental analogy of spiritual transformation. It would thus have been sensible for them to set up laboratory equipment in which they could, if they wished, conduct experiments which would be either straightforward or analogical.

We can take a modern example of the synchronistic way in which such external experiments can affect the psyche. A present-day alchemist describes an occasion when boiling a kettle for a cup of tea, in the midst of intense thought on the yoga of fire, which caused a psychological release within him at the precise time the kettle boiled, the external heating providing 'a kind of support to the inner work'.

Jung studied alchemy but failed to notice such occasions as this which would have illustrated synchronicity. Nevertheless, he did notice points of convergence between analytical psychology and alchemy. In particular, dream symbols and images had numerous parallels in alchemical literature. This discovery was very important to him for it underpinned his belief that there is in all of us a collective unconscious related to history and mythology. Further than that, it enabled him to see that alchemy had always had meaning for people in their search for self-development.

What he did not realize (or accept, if he did have such an intuition) was that there was in fact a physical change experienced in the successful alchemist: that a transmutation of substance did take place within the body. Taoists speak of a return to the state of the pliable infant as a description of the effects of the refinement of the physical energy in the body. Similarly, Paracelsus, the fourteenth century Swiss alchemist, spoke of 'The microcosm in its interior anatomy [having to] be reverberated up to the highest reverberation'. This is another clear reference to a fine tuning of energy. Jung saw this merely as an image of the fiery torment and purifying moral transformation that goes on in the individual.

He did not acknowledge that the transformation had a physical counterpart.

Throughout the world is this recognition that all manifested things (what Taoists call the ten thousand things) are emanations of the cosmic breath. Hippocrates referred to it, and John Dee, writing in 1564, set forward his idea of the 'monad' or unity underlying the universe. The monad represented the alchemic process and the goal of the alchemist, who in partaking of the Divine, took on the characteristics of God, and could thus redeem and transmute himself and his world.[4]

Man's true vocation has been and yet is to assist in the process of harmonization, to go with the flow, to be in accord with the yin and the yang as they are manifested in the changes visible all around. In all aspects of life this is true, no more so than in the study of alchemy.

Some hints as to method

First of all, it was important, as in such other sciences as feng shui and healing, that the stars and planets should be favourably placed, and the birth sign and time of the alchemist in good conjunction.

> To enter mountains one must secure a conjunction of the best season and day, on a day and at an hour that heaven holds in its grasp. Movement and rest should take place at the proper time as prescribed. Act according to the four seasons so as to suit the ch'i properly.[5]

Ch'i, as the vital breath of the universe, was fundamental to the process. An understanding of the cyclic transformations of the Five Elements was also necessary, and it is interesting that there are some parallels to this elsewhere in the world. For instance, Cooper quotes Alphidius who says:

> The Earth becomes liquid and is transformed into Water; Water becomes liquid and is transformed into Air; Air becomes liquid and is transformed into Fire; Fire becomes liquid and is transformed into glorified Earth, and this effect is what Hermes meant when he said in his secret: 'Thou shalt separate the earth from fire and the subtle from the dense.'[6]

While the yin and yang were peculiarly Taoist, the transmutation of elements as a cyclic process was a basic idea behind all alchemy. Such a cyclic picture was often symbolically represented by creatures swallowing their own tail: the dragon in the East, the serpent in the West. This cycle of change was found in the Tao returning to itself and to all aspects of nature through birth, death, and regeneration. It was logical for alchemists to find here a universal principle at work, one which it was legitimate and possible for man to explore and use, not only to help humans to fulfil themselves, but in order, as Taoists would put it, to maintain the Tao in being.

Ingredients varied from master to master, and were more often than not communicated in a highly coded form, but they generally included some or all of the following: cinnabar (sulphide of mercury), gold, silver, jade, pearls, mercury, and a plant identified as *chih*, and which could be sesame or a fungus. Mercury and silver were seen as yin metals, sulphur and gold as yang; the melting and melding of the yin and yang was a powerful means of releasing the energy of yin and yang, and thus of the ch'i. Ingredients that were occasionally used included sulphide of arsenic, mica, quartz, and various kinds of stalactite.

These substances clearly are real, and their use was in the cooking up of potions that would, it was hoped, confer immortality on those who ingested them. That many of them also had allegorical and symbolic meanings to do with internal transmutations is generally agreed.

Very often, no doubt, a combination was employed of internal alchemy and externally-produced potions, and in this cinnabar was a vital (and sometimes fatal) ingredient. Ground up, it provided the red pigment in painting and thus represents in symbolism and magic the energy of joined yin and yang. It was therefore a fundamental ingredient to alchemy. The energy generated by the combination of yin and yang (sulphur and mercury) was believed to accelerate the process of transforming ching into ch'i and ch'i into shen. So highly regarded was it, so necessary was it to the process, that it was often taken internally and premature death was often the paradoxical result of ingesting what was seen as a sure way to immortality.

Whatever the ingredients were, they generally had to be mixed in an iron cauldron and transmuted nine times over a period of nine days and nights without a break so that the activity of yin and yang could be released through a series of coagulations (yin) and meltings (yang).

Underlying alchemical methods worldwide is the idea of using the vital force to transmute the base physical body to a finer form, able to resonate with the energy of pure ch'i. More clearly than most, perhaps, it is the Taoist vision of this underlying cosmic energy which, by a variety of names in other parts of the world, is seen as the underlying energy at play in all forms of transmutation from the most mundane to the most ethereal. Most cultures had a belief in an afterlife or lives; it was only for the Chinese that it became important to link the evolution of the person with longevity or the achievement of immortality in this lifetime. This had the effect of clarifying objectives in their alchemists' minds. Indeed, it is perhaps in their essential pragmatism and refusal to separate the mundane from the ethereal, that Taoism can cast some light on the labrynth of writings on alchemy.

In the next chapter, we shall see how the Taoist belief in the identity of body and spirit as emanations of ch'i was translated into a unique form of alchemy in which all necessary ingredients were to be found within the body, mind, and relationships.

10.

Immortality: Dual Cultivation

We come now to an alchemy that is uniquely Chinese, aiming at immortality by transmutation of sexual fluids within the adept's body with the cooperation of a partner of the opposite sex: hence the name 'dual cultivation'.

What was aimed at is graphically illustrated in this quotation from a present day master, Huai-Chin Nan, in which there are shades of immortals flying the clouds:

> Merging with the cosmos is a necessary precondition for recognizing one's own spirit or divine self. This is what enables a person to advance. It enables one to condense shen and assemble ch'i, to project or refrain from projecting; to discern the size of the projected body, and to leave and return to the physical body at will... [1]

Whether this is true or not, Taoists have always believed that it was possible to attain immortality, or at least a good long life, by following certain alchemic practices, in one of which the cultivation of bodily ch'i played an important part and with which this chapter is concerned.

At this more mundane level, Taoists remind us that

> Essence, vitality and spirit continually interact. The sequence of their interaction in nature leads from void to form, from the universal to the particular, from the subtle to the gross. A sage is one who knows how to reverse this sequence, proceed backwards from gross to subtle, and thus regain original perfection for the substance or non-substance worked upon. [2]

It was long thought possible to refine through alchemy certain elements in such a way as to produce a draught, an elixir, or a Golden Pill that would produce immortality. The object in alchemy was to use the ch'i (which exists in all things animate and inanimate) to condense and dissolve the minerals to produce the Golden Pill or Flower. Alongside this went the spiritual and bodily alchemy with which this chapter is mainly concerned. The secrets of both forms of alchemy (if, indeed, there were two) were heavily guarded by symbolism, and it is often difficult to distinguish one from the other.

Tan Tao is the name of the school of Taoism devoted to immortals and immortality. It was and is concerned with methods of reversing the direction of the process of gradual loss through ageing of ching so that it becomes conserved and refined.

A hint of the method that enables this to happen is contained in one of its less cryptic sayings

> . . . if a man seizes for himself the secret forces of Heaven and Earth in order thereby to compound for himself the great elixir of the golden fluid, he will then exist coeval with Heaven and Earth from the beginning. . . Each time that Heaven unites itself with the Earth, seize for yourself the secret springs of the creative activities of yin and yang.[3]

Heaven and Earth, yang and yin, are here not very encoded words for male and female.

As it is said in *The Secret of the Golden Flower,*

> . . .we see that the ancients really attained long life by the help of the seed-energy present in their own bodies (and not by swallowing elixirs). . . when the right man makes use of wrong means, the wrong means work in the right way. By this is meant the transformation of seed into energy. But if the wrong man uses the right means, the right means work in the wrong way. By this is meant the bodily union of man and woman from which spring sons and daughters.[4]

Sex, therefore, is an important pathway to personal immortality, and not merely the pathway to species immortality.

Briefly, the process of alchemy in the body involves the transmutation of ching into ch'i, and the transmutation of ch'i into shen. The gross body in which the sexual energy is paramount is transformed to spirit, and the everyday differentiation into ching, ch'i and shen as aspects of the ten thousand things is no longer possible when all are returned to the state of the uncarved block.

Taoists see all phenomena as one, and as existing at various levels. As we have seen, ch'i can manifest in subtle and coarse forms. So can ching. In its coarse form it is male and female sex-

ual fluids. Like ch'i, it also has a subtle form. The processes leading to immortality involve a transmutation of the ching from its
gross and sexual aspect back to its immaterial and cosmic form.
Shen (spirit), too, suffers the same confusions, as it is not limited
to the religious meanings often associated with the word in the
West. It can mean the cosmic spirit, void, pure, undifferentiated
being, as much as it can refer to the spirit of life found within
the form of a single cell.

These three, ching, ch'i, and shen, are related in the process leading to immortality. The ching, by a process of refinement in which
ch'i is involved, transmutes to shen. It is clear that the subtle
aspects, at any rate, of all three are in most respects identical, as
all are of the Void.

But first, of course, the unruly coarse ching has to be controlled
and conserved. An anecdote illustrates this:

Huang Toi: 'I have heard that men of great antiquity lived over
two hundred years... But men of our time often die before they
reach the age of thirty...'

Su Ni: '(The reason) men often die young today is that they do
not know the secret of Tao. They are young and passionate and
they emit their ching indiscriminately when they love. It is like
cutting off the root and fountain of their lives... How can they
expect to live long?'[5]

Essential to success for men is retention of the semen. As Sun
S'su-mo recommends:

> For people in their twenties, one emission in four days... From the
> age of 60 upwards, emission should be avoided altogether; neverthe-
> less a 60-year-old who is still robust may permit himself one emis-
> sion a month, though by that age his thoughts should have long been
> tranquil and total abstention easy.[6]

The preservation of this yang essence strengthens the yang force
in man and brings him closer to heaven. But it is equally important that he continuously nourishes his yang essence with female
yin essence. This is why nearly all ancient Taoist texts stress the
importance of making love frequently and ejaculating infrequently.
Jolan Chang suggests jokingly that to make love ten times without
ejaculation would in itself lead to immortality!

So it follows that much of the literature and practical guidance
we see is to do with the control by the man of his ejaculation,
but it is also clear that the ching of a female partner is not only

essential to his success in this early stage of the process, but that the woman, too, needs the male essences if she is to succeed in attaining a to immortality.

Alongside the regulation of sexual activity go practices designed to restore and make good losses of ching. It is a counsel of perfection to say as Sun S'su-Mo does, 'When both partners are as spiritual as immortals, they can unite deeply without motion so that ching will not be stirred', yet that is the ideal.

Practices include the regulation of breathing, meditation, the regulation of the diet, the avoidance of strong emotion, and physical regimens such as the practice of T'ai Chi Ch'uan. 'Do not overwork your body; do not allow your vitality to become agitated. Then you will live long.' So said Kuang Ch'eng Tzu to Emperor Hwang Ti as reported by Chuang Tzu. It is worth comparing this to Chapter 16 of Tao Te Ching:

> Attain to the goal of absolute vacuity;
> Keep to the state of perfect peace.

Once this quieting has been achieved, including in the sex act, then it is possible for the subtle channels of ch'i to be opened. The central one, the Jen Mai, with its way stations, the three tan tien, is of particular importance.

By a secret yogic method, the male and female-derived ching are drawn up into the tan tien where the two are blended. Here ch'i is brought into the act, and the blend of ching is transmuted into ch'i and what is variously described as a spirit-embryo or golden pill is formed and thereafter drawn up the median psychic channel to be lodged in the ni-wan cavity close to the top of the skull.

However it is explained, whether in physiological, mystical or any other terms, what happens is quite clearly a very real and pronounced physical experience. A physiological description is given by Wen Kuan Chu thus: 'When the sex glands are active and one does not experience the slightest sexual desire, at that moment he is very close to real ching.' He or she may feel a

fulness in the middle palace stomach ch'i (which) will cause a sinking feeling. At this stage, if a man can clean his mind, wait quietly for spontaneous contractions of the testicles and perineum, or if a women experiences contractions of the uterus and reactions in the breast, and if he or she can dwell with those sensations for a while, a force will be produced which will move to the root of the nerves at the base of the spine.

'. . . he or she will (then) feel as if there is a line of force that moves through the inside of the pubis rushing up the lower tan tien, and meeting the ch'i which descends from the middle palace.'[7]

As Da Liu writes:

> The abdomen becomes as hot as fire, the ch'i rushes to the spine like steam. As it rises up the spine, it becomes more and more rarified until it reaches the head (the room of shen) where it produces a sensation of great emptiness and peace. As this emptiness spreads downwards, it condenses in the form of saliva, which appears in the rear of the mouth, is swallowed, and goes down to the abdomen where it is heated, starting the cycle all over again.[8]

This is the opening of the Jen Mai, the Central Channel. This opening, according to Wen Kuan Chu, will suddenly revive the activity of the youth gland or the abdomen, and a 'tremendous orgasm that exceeds sexual orgasm will occur. The orgasm will flow along the inner legs and feet and reach the soles of the feet and toes. At this time the joy and pleasure is like that experienced by a person who drinks good vintage wine. . .'

But this is apparently only the first stage of achievement in the transmutation of ching into ch'i. However, it is a crucial one, because it is said that if a person reaches it, then rejuvenation for a long time without illness is certainly possible.

Note the importance of the ch'i at this stage: the transmutation of ching into ch'i is the first barrier. Attention to the breathing continues, not because all ch'i is acquired from outside in this way, but so that the subtle ch'i residing in the body is stirred and thus enabled to play its part in the transmutation of both ching and shen. Attention to the breathing and the resulting consolidation of the ch'i should be continued, also, so that strong emotions may continue to be tranquillized.

The next stage is then approached, either by effort or spontaneously. More ch'i is generated and the whole body is said to begin a physical transformation in which the ching ch'i (the essential reproductive energy) causes the softer tendons and sinews to conduct the heat into the bones. When the lower spinal vertebrae are thus heated, they begin to sweat a liquid. When this cools it congeals, tightly sticking to the pores of the bones. In time, the bones fill up with this 'marrow' which on repeated cooling and heating will be consolidated into something as resilient as steel. 'The bones are now indestructible, tough, and resilient, not brittle or weak, but (strangely) as supple as an infant's. This is rejuvenation; at least the possibility of it.'[9]

As would be expected, the descriptions of further stages, that is of the transmutation of ch'i into shen and beyond, leave the physical sphere more and more, and partake of the language of mysticism, if only for reasons of secrecy. Certainly the end of the bodily process so far described is capable of attainment in other ways, for instance, through Ch'ang Ming diet.

In any case, whatever his route so far, a person is now enabled to gradually forget his bodily feelings when the eight extra meridians are open and fluent and the bones have acquired their steel-like resilience. For now comes the transmutation of ch'i into shen: when this, sometimes called the Development of the Golden Flower, is achieved, the middle barrier is passed and perfect stillness of heart supervenes. Immortality is within reach. 'The mind now shining with inner radiance is plunged within the stillness of the void.'[10] That there are few participants who actually reach even this stage, much less later ones, probably goes without saying.

What occurs is clothed in appropriately flowery language, such as: 'Three Flowers assemble on the top', and 'Five Ch'i go to the yuan'.

As to the first, ching, ch'i, and shen are the three flowers, and they have shot to the crown of the skull. 'The top of the head feels as if it is a high window with the sun shining upon it; it is open and clear as well as incomparably cool and pleasant.'[11]

As to the second, the five ch'i are the Five Elements in the form of heart, liver, spleen, lungs, and kidneys. The yuan is apparently either the tan tien or the perineum: 'Unless a real immortal appears and clarifies the matter, there is no obvious way in which we could settle this dispute. . .'[12]

Whatever the answer to this esoteric question, the phenomenon is accompanied by the person feeling his breath, including the breath of the lower tan tien, suddenly halting at about the time that the three flowers have assembled on the top. The entire body will become as soft as cotton and the person will feel warm and pleasant and be enjoying foetal breathing.

The state reminds me of those pleasant times of day when everything is calm and quiet. The mind and body, inside and outside,
heaven and earth, and everything else seems to occupy their own
centre or to be in a neutral position; this is a state of absolute peace
and harmony. One will not be conscious of his body or be aware
of either its existence or nonexistence. Ordinary thoughts and feelings disappear with a trace.[13]

After this, one naturally enters the stage of cultivating and nour-
ishing shen. Beyond this lie the higher reaches of what is now
quite definitely a spiritual endeavour, of the sort that is common to all traditions. It is another example of the old saying
about the innumerable paths that lead to the same mountain
summit.

No special practice is needed now. As a result of what has
gone before, the mind is ready to dissolve into the pure spirit of the
Void.

One has then acquired a body beyond a body; one is able to
leave this body at will and 'soar among the stars'. This flying is
a state of consciousness in which all sense of self and other, of
heaven and earth, has vanished: there is nought but pure void,
a limitless ocean of ch'i.

With the transmutation of shen into Void, the final barrier is
passed and immortality attained.

It seems to be one of the more exhausting means of climbing that
mountain. There are many stories of people, very intelligent and
very advanced in meditation techniques, who found no peace or
longevity, only madness.

Chuang Tzu tends to be dismissive of the art, and to hint that
its goal is a limited one, not commensurate with the effort involved:
'All this simply shows a desire for longevity', he says.

There are other ways up the mountain, he goes on: 'But as to
those. . . who attain to longevity without the management of the
breath, who forget all things and yet possess all things, whose
quietude is unlimited . . . such men pursue the Tao of heaven and
earth, and display the characteristics of the sages.'

There is the tale of a high government official who heard of
a Taoist who was over 200 years old, and who still looked young.
Asked the secret, the Taoist replied, 'I never approached a woman.'

That the disappointed official then asked what was the use of cultivating the Tao, is immaterial.

John Blofeld quotes The Green City Hermit: 'What is known as partaking of the golden pill does not signify bedroom arts, but drawing upon cosmic essence, vitality and spirit to add to one's own store.'[14]

There is a passage in *The Secret of the Golden Flower*:

> There is a tradition that the old Master P'eng grew to be eight hundred years old because he made use of serving maids to nourish his life, but that is a misunderstanding... In the Elixir of Life symbols are used for the most part, and in them the fire of the Clinging (li) is frequently compared to the bride, and the water of the Abyss to the boy ...From this arose the misunderstanding...[15]

It may be, then, that the sexual practices that are designed to conserve and transmute ching as the first step on the road to eternal life are no more to be regarded as statements of actual practice than are the stories of the alchemical creation of golden elixirs. The fact that either was accepted as true says more, perhaps, about the everyday interest of non-mystics than it does of the everyday life of mystics themselves.

11.

The Sage

Everyone has a way to follow, the way of his life. Herman Hesse writes:

> The life of every man is a way to himself, an attempt at a way, the suggestion of a path. No man has ever been utterly himself, yet every man strives to be so, the dull, the intelligent, each one as best he can.[1]

There are many difficulties, many byways to get lost in: benevolence, love of country, love of religion, intellectualism, the irresistible temptation to dissect, to find out, all leading to a cessation of the need to find contentment and sufficiency within.

The Tao Te Ching says:

> When the great Tao is lost, spring forth benevolence and righteousness.
> When wisdom and sagacity arise, there are great hypocrites.
> When family relations are no longer harmonious, we have filial children and devoted parents.
> When a nation is in confusion and disorder, patriots are recognised.
> Where Tao is, equilibrium is. When Tao is lost, out come all the differences of things.

This chapter is to do with self-sufficiency: the self-sufficiency of the Sage, the man of Tao.

The average man and woman have difficulty in finding contentment and sufficiency within their own beings and thus abandon their intrinsic nature in the pursuit of being something or someone else.

How to find the great Tao? He who undertakes this quest is known as the Sage, or to the Confucians as the Superior Man. Such a one is a fully realized man, though this concept takes us beyond the Western, Maslow-based model of the self-actualized, fully autonomous individual: 'the becoming fully human, the development of the fullest height that the human species can stand up to or that the particular individual can come to'.[2] This Western thought, while a welcome departure from the mainstream of psychological theory that preceded it, is to bring in comparisons, the differences of things. The truly autonomous man, the Sage, is one in whom the Tao acts without obstruction, his heart 'a placid lake unruffled by the winds of circumstance'.

Thomas Merton translates part of Chapter Six of Chuang Tzu as 'The True Man' and this gives the eastern view of unruffled yet cosmically powerful placidity:

What is meant by a 'true man'?
The true men of old were not afraid
When they stood alone in their views.
No great exploits. No plans.
If they failed, no sorrow.
No self-congratulation in success.
They scaled cliffs, never dizzy,
Plunged in water, never wet,
Walked through fire and were not burnt.
Thus their knowledge reached all the way
To Tao.
The true men of old
Slept without dreams,
Woke without worries.
Their food was plain.
They breathed deep.
True men breathe from their heels.
Others breathe with their gullets,
Half strangled. In dispute
They heave up arguments
Like vomit.

Where the fountains of passion
Lie deep
The heavenly springs
Are soon dry.

The true men of old
Knew no lust for life,
No dread of death.
Their entrance was without gladness,

Their exit, yonder, without resistance.
Easy come, easy go.
They did not ask where from,
Nor ask where to,
Nor drive grimly forward
Fighting their way through life.
They took life as it came, gladly;
Took death as it came, without care;
And went away, yonder,
Yonder!
They had no mind to fight Tao.
They did not try, by their own contriving,
To help Tao along.
These are the ones we call true men.

Minds free, thoughts gone
Brows clear, faces serene.
Were they cool? Only cool as autumn.
Were they hot? No hotter than spring.
All that came out of them
Came quiet, like the four seasons.[3]

The marks of a Sage are many, and include appropriateness of response, spontaneity, synchronous response, quietude, and others.

As regards the appropriateness of his or her behaviour: 'all that came out of them came quiet, like the four seasons.' The universe has endowed human beings with its very own nature, and living in accord with nature is the aim of the Sage. This principle of appropriateness is expressed, for example in the I Ching, as a way of balancing the yin and the yang, and a way of using energy, of relating the ch'i inside the man with the ch'i of the universe of which he is a part.

He is much concerned, then, with both the protection and the projection of his energy. This will be manifested appropriately in his daily life so long as he maintains a harmonious relation with the universe.

The Sage is not concerned with matters of right and wrong: he is concerned with harmony. Everyone's daily activities evoke responses throughout the universe which will be echoed back to them. So fortune and misfortune in one's life is self-created and results from the violation of this truth. The personal ch'i is a part of the universal ch'i: there is a two way response. This subtle universal energy resonates with a man's energy, and, depending on the energy he embodies, finds its expression in similar negative or positive events.

Behaviour in itself is neither right nor wrong: a situation exists in which the Sage seeks to operate harmoniously with the laws of nature, the five elements, and yin and yang. Questions to do with sin or virtue do not enter his calculations. If he thinks about the matter at all, he will regard sin as ignorance or madness since he knows that contravention of the laws of nature brings inevitable punishment. Sin, for the Taoist, is simply a violation of the harmony of the universe. What in theistic religions is an obligation to conform to the will of God is in Taoism a natural cooperation with the harmony of the universe. Animals and plants conform 'naturally'; only man chooses to maintain or destroy the balance.

So any suggestion that the Sage is not concerned with morals or ethics betrays a misunderstanding. There is no emphasis on morality because it is taken for granted; the stage of ethics has been surpassed.

> The mystical net of energy responses, also called destiny, is wide meshed, and the subtle energy does not necessarily respond immediately to the energy we project. But the principle of the universal law of subtle energy response applies to all of creation and extends its influence over the whole continuum of time and space and all its transformations.[4]

It is thus important for the Sage to be attentive to his ch'i. As Chuang Tzu says, 'You are trying to unify yourself, so you don't listen with your ears but with your heart (mind); you don't listen with your mind but with your spirit (ch'i)'.

> They had no mind to fight Tao.
> They did not try, by their own contriving,
> To help Tao along.
> These are the ones we call true men.

The mind, then, should be the servant of the ch'i which should

be the master over all aspects of a human being. Too often the
opposite prevails: the ch'i, being subdued by the mind, becomes
blind desire. But with harmony achieved, the Sage is able to react
directly even in the most difficult situations and can follow the
universal nature of productiveness and creativity rather than being
destructive.

Following the universal nature requires alertness and the ability
to relax. The Sage is therefore a master of wu wei. This word
literally means 'no action', but this is misleading if it gives the
impression of sitting around doing nothing like a clod of clay.
Just as 'Tao is ever inactive, yet there is nothing it does not do'
— so the Sage. He can be lively when necessary (though never
overstrained), and will act fully adequately when circumstances
demand it.

> I saw Demian's face and remarked that it was not a boy's face, but
> a man's and then I saw, or rather became aware, that it was not really
> the face of a man either; it had something different about it, almost
> a feminine element. And for the time being his face seemed neither
> masculine nor childlish, neither young nor old but a hundred years
> old, almost timeless and bearing the mark of other periods of his-
> tory than our own. Animals might look like this or trees or stars.[5]

Just as an animal in need of shade will, with relaxed ease, find
it, or a plant in need of sunshine will bend towards it, so the Sage
will do whatever is necessary easily and with just as much energy
as is necessary to perform it. He always has enough energy to
do what is necessary, because his whole life is based on the hus-
banding of his resources, of being in tune with the cosmic energies around him. He is therefore confident to do what most people
avoid: to trust to his own spontaneity in wu wei. Most people
avoid this. They prefer the seeming safety of a logical world-picture
with everything in its place labelled and categorized (to read books
to learn how to copulate, for instance). They prefer the seeming
safety of a set of social guidelines to lead them through the
labyrinth of social relationships. They avoid the unexpected and
upsetting and the need to adapt to the novel. They have cut themselves off from the natural supportive universe.

A practising Taoist makes the very important discovery that a
human being is not isolated, and is not a separate and unimport-
ant atom. Because the vital principle permeates everything, because
it flows through him and circulates through all of creation, he

experiences all aspects of life as interconnected and interrelated with the vast universe.

> In the dimension of time, what happens now is inevitably linked with the past and the future. In the dimension of space, everything one does either directly or indirectly influences the sphere of the universe to which one is connected, and a response appears in one's actions or mental projections.[6]

This being the case, it seems sensible to pick up the wavelength and cooperate with the universal power rather than to pursue activities that cause disharmony for oneself and others. By his daily practice, a Taoist Master is able to practice spontaneity that cooperates with the universe. Through such self-cultivation, such a person can serve himself and others. Taoists refine their energy until it becomes as subtle as the pivotal energy of the universe.

Such subtlety brings with it strange gifts, not least the ability to use the I Ching, for instance, to accurately predict change. Of Westerners, it was Jung who looked most deeply into this ability which had been recognized for centuries by the Chinese. In his own words, 'I therefore turned my attention to the intuitive technique for *grasping the total situation* which is so characteristic of China, namely the I Ching. . .'[7]. Jung detected in this, as well as in astrology and the events of ordinary life, what he called an 'acausal connecting principle' to be operating. He found that events and feelings were often clearly connected even when no obvious or direct causes and effects were apparent. It was more than mere coincidence: two events could often be clearly connected by more meaning than there was any right to expect using any logical, linear thought.

He called this principle *synchronicity*, 'a descriptive term for the link between two events that are connected through their meaning, a link that cannot be explained by cause and effect.'[8] (See also page 109.)

He found there were three types: (1) a coincidence between mental content (thought or feeling) and outer event, (2) a dream or vision which coincides with an event that is taking place at a distance, later verified, and (3) an image (dream, vision, or premonition) about something that will happen in the future, which then does occur.

When the coins are thrown or the yarrow stalks cast, the first of the three kinds of synchronicity is operating: what Jung and others are saying is that the total situation is involved, and that the prediction is synchronistically connected to the state of mind of the consulter. As Watts quite simply says, 'We assume that synchonicity exists when we consult the I Ching.' If we did not, there would be no point in consulting.

All of this is clearly connected to the response of the subtle energy of personal and cosmic ch'i referred to above. This subtle energy resonates with a man's energy, and, depending on the energy he embodies, finds its expression synchronistically in negative or positive events.

Jung pointed out that it was not only in the east that synchronicity was an accepted phenomenon. In a passage which is startling in its similarity to Taoist thinking, Hippocrates said:

> There is one common flow, one common breathing, all things are in sympathy. The whole organism and each one of its parts are working in conjunction for the same purpose... the great principle extends to the extremest part, and from the extremest part it returns to the great principle, to the one nature, being and not-being. The universal principle is found even in the smallest particle, which therefore corresponds to the whole.[9]

It is unsurprising, then, to find that the Sage, and to an extent, anyone who seeks to follow the Tao and to husband their ch'i, has an unusual skill in handling social affairs and practical matters. Such skill has been called 'coincidence control' and is typical of much of Chinese thinking and activity which is, wherever possible, a thinking in terms of the whole.

Chuang Tzu's story of 'The Master Woodcarver' ends, after a description of preliminary meditational practice, thus:

> By this time all thought of... `
> All that might distract me from the work
> Had vanished.
> I was collected in the single thought
> Of the bell stand.
>
> Then I went to the forest
> To see the trees in their own natural state.
> When the right tree appeared before my eyes,
> The bell stand also appeared in it, clearly,
>   beyond doubt.

All I had to do was to put forth my hand
And begin.

If I had not met this particular tree
There would have been
No bell stand at all.

What happened?
My own collected thought
Encountered the hidden potential in the wood;
From this live encounter came the work
Which you ascribe to the spirits.[10]

So, while the end product may flow, the preparation is the work
of a lifetime. Ni, Hua Ching outlines the Taoist lifestyle as consisting of eight basic foundations. These are: (1) early rising, (2)
early retiring, (3) the practice of serenity in sitting, (4) the practice of serenity in moving, (5) heeding one's words, (6) the
avoidance of excessive sexual activity, (7) the avoidance of excessive indulgence in foods, and (8) the abstinence from engagement
in unnecessary activities.

Building on these foundations would be the practices of controlling ch'i through breathing exercises and meditation in action
(T'ai Chi Ch'uan).

But above and beyond these, there would be the concentration
on quietude. The Sage's object is to return to the uncarved block,
the original state of his or her being. For this, one has to become
a master of stillness. 'In repose [he] shares the passivity of the
yin, in action the energy of the yang.'[11] So said Chuang Tzu, to
whom excesses of any kind were anathema, 'Exhaling and inhaling, getting rid of the old, assimilating the new, stretching like
a bear and craning like a bird — this is but valetudinarianism,
affected by professors of hygiene and those who try to preserve
the body to the age of P'eng Tsu.'[12]

The Tao Te Ching, chapter 52, says:

Thus, however his body may decay, he will never perish.
If he shuts his mouth and closes his doors,
He can never be exhausted.
If he opens his mouth and increases his affairs,
He can never be saved.
To see the minuteness of things is called clarity of sight;

To keep to what is weak is called power.
Use your light, but dim your brightness;
Thus you will cause no harm to yourself.
This is called following the eternal.

As Eugen Herrigel says, 'Man is a thinking reed but his great works are done when he is not calculating and thinking. Childlikeness has to be restored...'[13]

They had no mind to fight Tao.
They did not try, by their own contriving,
To help Tao along.
These are the ones we call true men.

But it is this restoration of childlikeness, the discovery of one's face before one is born, the journey back to the uncarved block — it is this subtle process that is so difficult as to be almost self-defeating. When, after long years of training, so well described by Herrigel, the art of self-forgetfulness is attained, 'man thinks yet he does not think. He thinks like the showers coming down from the sky; he thinks like the waves rolling on the ocean... indeed he is the showers, the ocean...'

This spontaneity is the highest principle in Taoist cultivation and life. 'After a man evolves to the absolute level of being, his breathing may cause wind, his sneeze a rain storm, his anger a fire, and his shaking an earthquake. He is one with the Tao.'[14]

12.

The Union of Hemispheres

There are two main thrusts to this chapter, which sets out to demonstrate that the concept of ch'i is not one that is confined to the mystic East, but is a part of the underlying beliefs of the hard-headed West. Indeed, it will be a demonstration that the two hemispheres are drawing closer again.

> By our insistence that the scientific method is the only means by which anything can be known, doors of perception are closed, the wisdom of the East is denied us, and our own inner world becomes one-sided. East and West are two halves of a whole; they represent the two inner aspects of each individual man and woman. The psychological split needs healing through an inner union, allowing flow between left and right hemispheres, between scientific and spiritual, masculine and feminine, yang and yin.[1]

A comparison between the right and left hemispheres of the human brain and the East and West hemispheres of the planet may be far-fetched. Nevertheless, it has long been known in psychology that loss of creativity on the one hand is caused by cutting off from consciousness the contents of the right (east) hemisphere, just as a loss of rationality is caused by a cutting off of the left (west) hemisphere. It may be that a re-harmonisation of the planet is in prospect through a kind of global leaderless therapy.

The first aspect of this potential union that will be under consideration will be the parallels between ch'i and some insights gained from modern physics.

The second aspect will be a consideration of the implications stemming from Jung's concept of synchronicity.

Underlying all, will be a consideration of the way in which the

West appears to be waking to the fact that it may have taken a wrong path in trying to separate man from the rest of the universe.

Modern Physics

As regards the first topic, the parallels between Eastern and Western thought in the matter of ch'i, it is true to say that relevant Western thought has been focussing on the minute, on sub-atomic particles, on top of which the rest of the material world seems to roll on unchanged. It has always been thus: the lamas in far Tibet and the Zennists in Zazen have had their insights while empires rise and crumble around them. What is happening is that those insights are now being shared by some of the foremost Western-style scientists. They agree now with the mystics and philosophers of East (and West) that the whole basis of our material world does appear to rest on extremely transient phenomena. Phenomena, indeed that appear at first sight to be activated by no possible rhyme nor reason.

It appears, according to Capra, that particles can be created out of the Void: that is quite literally out of nothing, from a physical vacuum, and can disappear in a similar manner. Furthermore, he claims that such events happen 'all the time'. He goes on to say:

> Like the Eastern Void, the 'physical vacuum' as it is called in field theory is not a state of mere nothingness, but contains the potentiality for all forms of the particle world. These forms in turn are not independent physical entities but merely transient manifestations of the underlying Void... the vacuum is truly a 'living void', pulsing in endless rhythms of creation and destruction... From its role as an empty container of the physical phenomena, the void has emerged as a dynamic quantity of utmost importance.[2]

Truly, the void has emerged in western physics as of utmost importance, and from our point of view, the 'dynamic container' can be regarded as the Tao, and its endless rhythms of creation and destruction as manifestations of the ch'i.

> '...When one knows that the Great Void is full of ch'i, one realizes that there is no such thing as nothingness.'[3]

A picture is emerging of a world that is wholly non-material, a world that is basically not of matter. Instead, there are patterns of energy (ch'i) that are eternally moving and changing. It is a picture of particles that can turn into waves, travel backwards in time, and disappear into the void.

The whole thing has been likened, and not only by Capra, to a dance, 'where space and time are aspects of a continuum and an underlying pattern of oneness seems to exist'.[4]

This is a picture that has been commonly held in the East, in Hinduism and Buddhism as well as in Taoism. It was also a picture less commonly expressed in the West, for instance by Hippocrates, when he wrote in 'De Alimento' of 'one common flow, one common breathing... the greatest principle extends to the extremest part, and from the extremest part it returns to the great principle, the one nature, being and not-being'.[5]

It is Capra, of modern physicists, who draws the closest parallels between the notion of ch'i and the notion of the quantum field. He points out that the idea of ch'i, at any rate as conceived of by neo-Confucians, is one of a 'tenuous, non-perceptible form of matter'. This, they said, was present throughout the universe, and could condense to form material things. It breathed and was subject to cyclic periodicity: all forms would eventually return to the Void. It is worth noting here that Heraclitus of Ephesus, dubbed by Capra 'the Greek Taoist', not only emphasized a principle of continuous change, like Lao Tzu, but put forward the view that all such changes have a cyclic character as expressed in the working of the I Ching and the Theory of the Five Elements.

Capra quotes from Walter Thirring and Joseph Needham:

Modern theoretical physics... has put our thinking about the essence of matter in a different context. It has taken our gaze from the visible — the particles — to the underlying entity, the field. The presence of matter is merely a disturbance of the perfect state of the field at that place; something accidental, one could almost say, merely a 'blemish'. Accordingly, there are no simple laws describing the forces between elementary particles... Order and symmetry must be sought in the underlying fields.

The Chinese physical universe in ancient and medieval times was a perfectly continuous whole. Ch'i condensed in palpable matter was not particulate in any important sense, but individual objects acted and reacted with all other objects in the world... in a wave-like or vibratory manner dependent, in the last resort, on the rhythmic alternation at all levels of the two fundamental forces, the yin and the yang. Individual objects thus had their intrinsic rhythms. And these were integrated... into the general pattern of the harmony of the world.[6]

Again, there is a picture of dynamic interrelationships tending towards harmony.

Such a process is that underlying the theory of the Five Elements and also the I Ching. In the latter, the hexagrams arranged in their proper order illustrate symbolically the entire sequence of changes which everything in the universe undergoes, from virtual particles with life expectancies of a billionth of a second, to galaxies, with life expectancies of billions of years.

However, man is a part of the total, and increasingly interferes with the harmony in this minute corner of the universe and thereby loses harmony with his fellows and within himself. Some men and women realize this and try to reintegrate themselves with the universe. By relating his affairs to parts of the I Ching sequence, a man can forecast with great accuracy how his affairs will prosper or decline. Sometimes, such foreknowledge can be used to advantage, but always the consulter is advised to 'accord gracefully' with changes, thus maintaining the underlying harmony of the universe. Thus may man reintegrate himself and restore cosmic harmony.

It is interesting that Capra draws a parallel between the I Ching and the S-Matrix of quantum physics. The S (or Scattering) matrix is to do with prophesying the fate of particles in collision. In this there is no possibility of prophesying certainties, but only of probabilities, tendencies, or processes. He points out that this is just what happens in I Ching divination; no certainties, but possible outcomes themselves subject to coming change. But Capra is at pains to point out that such parallels as these are not of fundamental importance. What is of importance, he feels, is the parallel between this modern Western and traditional Chinese thinking that it is change and transformation that is the primary feature of the universe, and that it is the structures and symmetries generated by those changes that are secondary.

Another fundamental parallel between the thinking generated by quantum physics and traditional Chinese thought — indeed, with Eastern thought in general — is that objectivity is an impossibility. It is quite clear that man is not able to stand outside and observe dispassionately and objectively. His very presence, the very fact that he is observing, affects that which he observes. Similarly, that which he observes affects him. Eastern thought sees men as integral to the universe, no more important nor less important than anything else. Furthermore, as a part of it, he is involved in it, and it in him. He is a part of nature studying itself. This insight is shared by many western scientists, including quantum physicists and people such as Carl Jung, the psychologist who has done so much to bridge the gap, in every sense, between the two hemispheres.

Synchronicity

One of his great contributions was to put forward the theory of the 'collective unconscious', shared by all men everywhere.

Related to this is his work on what he came to call synchronicity (see also page 101). This was the word he gave to a phenomenon he observed in his clinical work as well as in his study of the I Ching and related matters. Very often events and feelings were clearly related, but not by any obvious or direct linking cause. He cites as an example from clinical work the time when a patient was telling him of a dream in which an Egyptian Golden Scarab had figured; at the same time there had been a knocking on the window which had been caused by the nearest kind of European beetle to a Golden Scarab. This, and similar cases went, he believed, beyond the merely coincidental. He believed that there was a connection between synchronistic events and the workings of the collective unconscious.

His friend, the quantum physicist, Pauli, also believed that parapsychological phenomena including apparent coincidences were the visible traces of an underlying, untraceable principle in the universe.

Both men were aware of an interrelationship that often blurred the boundaries between people and between events. Jung did much work on parapsychology and astrology, and found examples of an acausal principle at work with accompanying synchronistic events in evidence.

As Jean Bolen remarks, 'With the idea of synchronicity, psychology joined hands with parapsychology and theoretical physics in seeing an underlying "something" akin to what the mystic has been seeing all along. . . Theories and laboratory experiences make thinkable the idea of an underlying invisible connection between everything in the universe.'[7]

Synchronicity describes the links that are often found between two events that are connected through meaning and not by cause and effect.

This 'meaning', this 'underlying, untraceable principle of the universe', is interesting in our context, because of the link that Jung made with the processes at work in operating the I Ching. One of the three types of synchronicity he found was 'a coincidence between mental content (thought or feeling) and an outer event'. This seems to be an excellent account of what goes on in divination.

The I Ching is to do with the processes of change; change is related to the Five Elements; the Five Elements are aspects of ch'i. The I Ching is thus to do with ch'i and its changes. Such changes manifest themselves both causally and acausally: in clear terms of cause and effect and also in terms of synchronistic events. There is a clear causal connection between chemotherapy and cure of cancerous tissue, but (at any rate to Western eyes) an acausal connection between an acupuncture point, a needle, and relief of disease.

In ch'i, then, may be found the 'untraceable principle' that Pauli wistfully wrote of.

Jung writes:

> No serious investigator would assert that the nature of what is observed to exist, and of that which observes, namely the psyche, are known and recognized quantities. If the latest conclusions of science are coming nearer and nearer to a unitary idea of being, characterized by space and time on the one hand and by causality and synchronicity on the other, that has nothing to do with materialism. Rather it seems to show that there is some possibility of getting rid of the incommensurability between the observed and the observer. The result, in that case, would be a unity of being which would have to be expressed in terms of a new conceptual language — a 'neutral language', as Pauli once called it.[8]

But such a conceptual language already exists. It is a language of science, albeit an eastern science, that has discovered over the centuries principles that were for centuries at odds with the principles that Western science was coming up with.

> The intention of the Taoist sciences is to demonstrate the identicalness of metaphysical and physical phenomena, the oneness of the reality of matter, the oneness of spirituality and ordinariness in our life. The human mind created duality, but, through the Taoist knowledge and practices, one may reintegrate the apparent dualities in one's life and experience oneness.[9]

Western science, on the other hand, is concerned with duality and causality. It has been bedevilled by the object/subject dichotomy. It has tended to be left-hemisphered, with the use of logic and linear thinking, an insistence on measurement and replicability. Eastern science has been concerned with oneness and admission of acausality. It has tended to be right-hemisphered, and to be concerned with wholes rather than parts, tolerance of ambiguity, to use intuition, and to see man as an integral part of the universe.

The global village concept must lead to a greater appreciation by each hemisphere of the other: this can be seen in the field of medicine where Chinese doctors use western surgery as well as traditional methods, and Western medics use holistic healing, acupuncture and so on in at least a marginal way. A link between the two hemispheres is coming about, but on an ad hoc basis. A principle is needed.

It would be a large claim to say that ch'i is such a linking principle between the two hemispheres, but at least it is an aspect of man's thinking that is worth consideration in the West, particularly when linked with the respectability of quantum physics and, it must be said, with the insights of western mystics and philosophers old and new.

For it is not necessarily a new idea in the West: it has just been buried beneath the pile of words and ideas of the science that has appeared since Bacon. Apart from such as Hippocrates and Heraclitus already mentioned, the link between western theory and the concept of ch'i and the Tao is still being made. Weiss-kopf, for instance:

> Man experiences everything in terms of a dialectical trinity, consisting of a basic antinomy, a polarity of the two antinomic poles (Two), and an ultimate unity of the two. . . This polarity is the intermediate link between the antinomy (One) and the ultimate unity (Three) of the two poles. They're only different aspects of something which is ontologically one. This trinity is most lucidly symbolized by the sign of the Tao in Chinese philosophy, by the two intertwined halves in black and white, included in the union of the circle (Three).[10]

David Bohm, too, with his work written up in his book, 'Wholeness and the Implicate Order', prefers to start with the whole, oneness, in contradistinction to many Western scientists, who, as we have seen, start with the idea of parts and see how they fit together.

The most fundamental level, according to Bohm, is 'that which is', an unbroken wholeness. All things, space, time, matter, and anti-matter, are forms of that which is. Even non-being is a form of that which is, which makes it very difficult for Westerners to deal with 'that which is' in any logical manner. Bohm, like Jung and Pauli before him, calls for a new language, a new instrument of thought.[11]

Such a new instrument exists, of course, and has done so for some thousands of years, based on the Tao, on that which is, on unbroken wholeness, and on the Tao's instrument of creation and destruction, rhythm and harmony: **CH'I**.

Conclusion

We — you, individual reader, and I, individual writer — will live out our lives in our separate ways. Or so it will seem to us.

Yet we are linked, you and I, both subject to the flow of ch'i within and without us.

Even if we had never met through these words, it is still true that the ways in which we channel our ch'i will affect each of us, will affect the balance of our neighbourhood, our world, and ultimately the cosmos. We are at the same time both minute and ephemeral and of fundamental importance and eternal worth in the scale of things.

We should practise letting go, wu wei, in order to better attune ourselves to the flow of ch'i (as well as to prolong our lives).

That light is somehow better than darkness and that good is certainly preferable to evil is an article of Western faith. From this springs our drive to conquer what is seen as evil, and forcibly to change the world for what is often merely a temporary advantage. Yet ch'i, cosmic and therefore universal energy, manifesting itself in yin and yang, appears in all opposites. The two are inseparable, and good needs evil for its existence, as light needs darkness: the one cannot exist without the other. In the one is the seed of the other, as we can clearly see in the yin/yang symbol (Figure 5).

Characteristic of the east, particularly of the ancient Chinese way of life known as Taoism, is the knowledge that good cannot exist without evil, nor light without darkness. Followers of Taoism have their article of faith, too: the cosmos, constantly changing, depends on a delicate maintenance of a balance of opposites. Everything, including the bad, the dark, and the negative, has a necessary part to play.

As long as we are alive, we are subject to change, and to the

Figure 5: *The Yin/Yang symbol, each half containing the seed of its opposite.*

need to retain a dynamic balance in our lives. To change is to upset the balance of what is. As in the act of walking, the tendency to fall forward must be balanced by an opposite tendency. The process is continual and cyclic — not linear, irreversible, and entropic.

The Chinese do not see any process of entropy: any apparent decline is only the dark side of a cyclic process which will lead to bright birth. A martial artist will be careful, for example, to balance any advance with a corresponding retreat. In martial arts, geomancy, healing, and the pursuit of wisdom, we have seen how the Taoist seeks out the harmony of opposites by careful attention to the flow of ch'i as manifested in the interplay of yin and yang.

Their constant interplay maintains atoms and galaxies in being.

In between is man, and in his pursuits yin and yang should be given full expression. As in martial arts, those dances of the warrior, we have seen how strength should be balanced by weakness, advance by retreat, upward movement by downward, and have seen how this concept can be applied to all phenomena and activities. The complementary forces cement the manifest world, for it is in their balancing act that it is maintained in being.

It is hardly necessary to catalogue the disastrous effects of our present one-sided yang attack on the natural world. It is characteristic of this approach that the yin is largely discounted, so that the beneficient flow of ch'i is impeded.

Yet Nature moves always towards balance. From the maintenance of satellites in their orbits to the maintenance of the structure of individual atoms is seen the play of yin and yang. An ancient Chinese text says: 'Yin/yang is the way of heaven and earth, the fundamental principle of the myriad things, the father and mother of change and transformation, the root of inception and destruction'.

All beings and things, all systems, natural and man-made, are in a state of dynamic change, tension, and coexistence which is unceasing. Since we are part of the process whether we like it or not, we are wise to avoid destroying the harmony by over-enthusiasm, exploitation, and competitiveness. Instead we should look for and aid the inevitable process of harmony. Otherwise we could find ourselves squeezed out as dispensable to the system, as the yin and yang work towards the harmonious flow of ch'i. This process can be seen at work around us in the tensions between tendencies towards global disaster and global cooperation. Daily headlines are proof enough.

We may leave aside the obvious examples evident in the arms race. Other examples abound. The production of butter mountains, for instance, is balanced by famine, and this phenomenon in itself tends towards harmony as a growing number of people seek a remedy. Similarly, the concentration of capital in the developed nations is balanced by the indebtedness of the third world and a gradual growth in accompanying insight. The likely crash of western economies is only the natural progression from bull to bear, from male dragon to submissive female tiger, from thrusting yang to retreating yin. It too, the Taoists would say, will lead to a return to a balance — before yet another cycle begins.

Even in our painting and poetry there is a search for rest and balance. A work of art is successful when it exhibits and communicates a sense of rest within tension, in so far as it involves the individual member of the audience in finding that release of tension within his own psyche. Taoists, more consciously than our own artists, perhaps, seek to put qualities of yin and yang into juxtaposition so that each balances and influences the other. They balance darkness and solidity with light and emptiness: it is in the eye and ear of the beholder to feel the vitality apparent in the contrived tension.

Just so are all natural phenomena maintained in creative tension by the play of the yin and the yang. Humanity should go along with this. How can we hope to resist a system that is cosmic?

The Tao of Politics
Western states, economies, and governments are constantly in a state of upheaval. Headlines attest, for instance, to winters of discontent.

James Callaghan, former British Prime Minister, once spoke of politics having a cycle of thirty years. He recognized, as all politicians do, that he was operating in a changing world; he recognized that change is the essence of life. Where he differed from most of his fellows was in seeing change as cyclic.

It is an awareness of inevitable change that motivates politicians, sooner or later in their cycle of power, to attempt radical change. Taoists would say that if a person finds himself in a position of power, he should try to do as little as possible, leaving the balance to be achieved by the yin and the yang, twin controllers of change. But, alas, the average politician, male or female, becomes an exponent of the masculine, yang, rationalizing drive for power at the expense of the gentler yin element.

Remember, however, that hidden in the yang is always the seed pearl of its opposite. In any rational plan devised by a human being there will be a certain amount of irrationality stemming, perhaps, from unconscious drives within. Similarly, in any wildly extravagant scheme, there will be a trace of rationality, merely because it has been devised by a human for a human need. In those seed-pearls are hidden the beginnings of unexpected changes, changes that sometimes thwart the planner, but which are tendencies towards dynamic cosmic balance.

One aspect of change is conflict: conflict between what is and that which is being born out of what is. Politicians are either good at managing change and conflict or they are not. Much of their energy goes into persuasion and resisting persuasion.

Taoists, by contrast, say that the best way of controlling change is to flow with it. The wise politician is he or she who, in the words of Lao Tsu, governs a state like cooking a small fish: very carefully, very lightly.

The ideal ruler, according to Lao Tzu, shares with his fellows the understanding that change is inevitable, and that anything done is destined to have only a marginal effect on the world and its evolution. Such a leader, knowing this, will, like Chuang Tzu dragging his tail in the mud,[1] be unwilling to seek office: such a leader is more likely to find himself in power by virtue of the people's trust in him. It is hard to think of such a person in the world today.

The Tao Te Ching is full of sound, if unwelcome, advice to the politician. As chapters 57 and 58 have it:

> The more laws and restrictions there are
> The poorer people become. . .
> The more rules and regulations,
> The more thieves and robbers.
> When the country is ruled with a light hand
> The people are simple.
> When the country is ruled with severity,
> The people are cunning.

In other words, the natives become restless and seek to outwit their masters. The results are secrets trials, neighbour encouraged to spy on neighbour, big fraud in high places, little fraud in low places, muzzling of media, and so on: the list is elastic. But the wise politician, like the retired Callaghan, will remember that change is cyclic. Any overreaching of the yang, positive, thrusting power of the politician with a mandate and a subservient following will inevitably be followed by a yin-like loss of power. Like the boy with his finger in the dyke, such ruling cliques or despots (even the benevolent) cannot forever stem the flow of rebelliousness, bolshiness, or seasons of discontent.

In all opposites are found yin and yang. In all conflict is found the dynamic balance between the two. Hidden like a jewel in the centre of any conflict, from family disagreement to industrial dispute to Northern Ireland to European farm prices to ballistic missile treaty difficulties, is its resolution.

Small comfort to people beset by the seemingly inexorable march of big business, agribusiness, nuclear energy, and engines of war. Nevertheless, we may find cautious comfort in the enigmatic Taoist belief that everything contains seeds of its own inevitable cyclic change.

Lao Tzu would advise politicians to move with the tide. Like good martial artists, they should give way willingly and lovingly where there is pressure in order to be able to advance positively and lovingly in the new direction leading to their ultimate goal.

In such a way a spring of discontent could bring forth a harvest of content.

> A good soldier is not violent,
> A good fighter is not angry,
> A good winner is not vengeful,
> A good employer is humble.
> This is known as the virtue of not striving.
> This is known as the ability to deal with people.
>
> Tao Te Ching, Chapter 68

The politician who wishes to advance and become a statesman, is thus exhorted to follow the flow of ch'i, to exercise wu wei, to take life easy. Former President Reagan is a case in point: notorious for his unwillingness to think very deeply about anything, for his unwillingness to take his work home with him, his penchant for trusting his gut feelings: who is to say whether he was a worse president for all that? Who is to say whether history will judge him to have been successful? After all, there were the yang-merchants, the Oliver Norths, redressing the balance. In the light of history, Reagan will probably stand out no further than the more energetic of his contemporaries. Thatcher, Kohl, Hawke: their names will be vaguely remembered as some sort of politician.

Another leader, Churchill (a manic depressive, alternating between yang and yin in his personal life), who rallied his country in war by powerful yang, needed the yin-like strengths of ordinary people in his country to suffer uncomplainingly, discover neighbourliness, and to toil for few rewards for his success.

This concluding section has concentrated on politicians to a great extent, for it seems that in this day and age, as in most others, our fate is very much in their hands.

But is it? Although evil must often appear to stalk the land, its opposite, great goodness, is always there, balancing. If this were not so, the human race would have perished long ago. The influence of yin and yang in the flow of the cosmic energy in which we are all sustained sees to it that dynamic balance is maintained.

A search for harmony and balance in all aspects of their lives and their environment is a constant preoccupation of Taoists. They pursue a way of life that is based on rhythm and flux, of flowing with things, watching the interplay of yin and yang around and in them. Such people tend to be poets, artists, mystics — and scientists, too. What else but science is the application of natural principles to health and well-being?

So they pursue a life-style which could not be further from materialism. Worry and ambition are kept to a minimum. It is a life-style in which beds may be moved in order to observe without interruption the gradual blossoming, unfolding, and death of a single bloom.

Notes

Chapter 1:
1. John Blofeld, *Taoism: the Quest for Immortality*, Ch.10.
2. Chang Chung-yuan, *Creativity and Taoism*, p.63ff.
3. Chang Chung-yuan, op. cit., p.65.
4. *Tao Te Ching*, Ch.1.
5. John Blofeld, op. cit., p.147.
6. Chang Chung-yuan, op. cit., p.138.

Chapter 2:
1. Ni, Hua Ching, *Tao*, p.24.
2. J.C. Cooper, *Yin and Yang*, p.53.
3. Stephen Skinner, *The Living Earth Manual of Feng Shui*, p.55.
4. Confucius, *The Great Appendix to the I Ching*.

Chapter 3:
1. J.C. Cooper, *Chinese Alchemy*, p.98.
2. D.L. Overmyer, *Religions of China*, p.49.
3. D.C. Lau, *The Analects*, p.54.
4. H.A. Giles, *Chuang Tzu*, p.308.
5. J.C. Cooper, *Yin & Yang*, p.31.

Chapter 4:
1. Aleister Crowley, *Magick Without Tears*.

2. Da Liu, *The Tao and Chinese Culture*, p.67.
3. Laszlo Legeza, *Tao Magic*, p.13.
4. Ko Hung, *Pao P'u Tzu*, quoted by Legeza, op. cit., p.13.
5. Sarah Rosbach, *Feng Shui*, Appx.5.
6. Laszlo Legeza, op. cit., p.22.
7. ibid, p.19.
8. ibid, p.62.
9. Ni, Hua Ching, op. cit., p.132.

Chapter 5:

1. Eugen Herrigel, *Zen in the Art of Archery*, p.102
2. *Tao Te Ching*, Ch.42.
3. Chang Chung-yuan, op. cit., p.211.
4. J.C. Cooper, *Taoism*, p.96.
5. Alan Watts, *Tao, the Watercourse Way*, p.29.
6. Jean Bolen, *The Tao of Psychology*, p.9.
7. Chang Chung-yuan, op. cit., p.211.
8. ibid, p.212.
9. Alan Watts, op. cit., p.15.
10. J.C. Cooper, op. cit., p.100.
11. Rawson & Legeza, *Tao*, p.10.
12. Alan Watts, op. cit., p.15.
13. J.C. Cooper, *Yin and Yang*, p.61ff.
14. Chang Chung-yuan, op. cit., p.213.

Chapter 6:

1. Ni, Hua ching, op. cit., p.78.
2. Ralston. p.29
3. Shakti Gawain, *Creative Visualization*, p.13.
4. Joe Hyams, *Zen in the Martial Arts*, p.84.
5. Ralston. p.27
6. Lo et al, *The Essence of T'ai Chi Ch'uan*, p.75.
7. Jo Hyams, op. cit., p.66.
8. Ni, Hua Ching, op. cit., Ch.6.
9. ibid, p.65ff.

Chapter 7:
1. Chee Soo, *Taoist Ways of Healing,*, p.26.
2. Ni, Hua Ching, op. cit. p.35.
3. Tao Te Ching, Ch.64.
4. Chee Soo, op. cit. p.111.
5. Laszlo Legeza, op. cit., p.26ff.
6. Wen-shan Huang, *The Fundamentals of T'ai Chi Ch'uan*, p.487.
7. Chee Soo, *Taoist Yoga* p.44
8. Chee Soo, *Taoist Ways of Healing*, p.48ff.
9. Ni, Hua Ching, op. cit., p.65ff.

Chapter 8:
1. Sarah Rosbach, op. cit., p.21.
2. ibid, p.24.
3. Stephen Skinner, op. cit., p.19.
4. ibid, p.38.
5. ibid, p.102.
6. E.J. Eitel, *Feng Shui*, p.50.

Chapter 9:
1. J. Needham, *Science and Civilization in China*, vol.5, pt.2, passim.
2. Chee Soo, *Taoist Ways of Healing*, Ch.13, passim.
3. Blofeld, *Taoism*, p.14
4. J. Dee, *The Hieroglyphic Monad*, passim.
5. Cooper, *Chinese Alchemy*, p.87.
6. ibid, p.93.

Chapter 10:
1. Wen Kuan Chu, *Tao and Longevity*, p.109.
2. John Blofeld, op. cit., p.116.
3. Chang Chung-yuan, op., cit., p.134.
4. Richard Wilhelm, *The Secret of the Golden Flower*, p.63.
5. Jolan Chang, *The Tao of Love and Sex*, p.126.
6. ibid, p.74.

7. Wen Kuan Chu, op. cit., p.94ff.
8. Da Liu, *The Tao and Chinese Culture*, p.95ff.
9. Wen Kuan Chu, op. cit., p.94.
10. John Blofeld, op. cit., p.149.
11. Wen Kuan Chu, op. cit., p.104.
12. ibid, p.103.
13. ibid, p.104ff.
14. John Blofeld, op. cit., p.133.
15. Wilhelm, op. cit., p.62.

Chapter 11:
1. Herman Hesse, *Demian*, p.8.
2. Abraham Maslow, *The Farther Reaches of Human Nature*, p.162.
3. Thomas Merton, *The Way of Chuang Tzu*, p.60ff.
4. Ni, Hua Ching, op. cit., p.101.
5. Herman Hesse, op. cit., p.49.
6. Ni, Hua Ching, op. cit., p.107ff.
7. C.G. Jung, *Synchronicity*, p.49.
8. Jean Bolen, op. cit., p.14.
9. C.G. Jung, op. cit., p.101.
10. Merton, op. cit., p.101.
11. Giles, *Chuang Tzu*, p.143.
12. ibid, p.152.
13. Engen Herrigel, op. cit. p.7.
14. Ni, Hua Ching, op. cit., p.107.

Chapter 12:
1. Jean Bolen, op. cit., p.9.
2. Fritjof Capra, *The Tao of Physics*, p.235.
3. ibid, p.235.
4. ibid, Ch.15, passim.
5. Jung, op. cit., p.101.
6. Capra, op. cit., p.225.
7. Bolen, op. cit., p.84.
8. Jung, op. cit., p.133.
9. Ni, Hua Ching, op. cit., p.101.

10. Quoted by Siti Salamah, 'Systems Methodologies &
    Isomorphies', p.35ff.
11. David Bohm, *Unfolding Meaning*, passim.

Conclusion
1. Giles, *Chuang Tsu*, p.170.

Bibliography

Blofeld, John. *Taoism* (Unwin, 1979).

Bolen, Jean S. *The Tao and Psychology* (Wildwood House, 1980).

Capra, Fritjof. *The Tao of Physics* (Fontana, 1976).

Chang Chung-yuan. *Creativity and Taoism* (Wildwood House, 1975).

Chang, Jolan. *The Tao of Love and Sex* (Granada, 1979).

Chee Soo. *Taoist Yoga* (Aquarian Press, 1983).

Chee Soo. *Taoist Ways of Healing* (Aquarian Press, 1986).

Chu Ta-kao. *Tao Te Ching* (Unwin, 1976).

Cooper, Jean C. *Taoism* (Aquarian Press, 1972).

Cooper, Jean C. *Yin and Yang* (Aquarian Press, 1981).

Cooper, Jean C. *Chinese Alchemy* (Aquarian Press, 1984).

Da Liu. *The Tao of Health and Longevity* (Routledge Kegan Paul, and Associated Book Publishers [UK] Ltd, 1979).

Da Liu. *The Tao and Chinese Culture* (Routledge Kegan Paul, 1981).

Dee, John. *The Hieroglyphic Monad* (Samuel Weiser, 1975).

Eitel, E.J. *Feng Shui* (Pentacle, 1979).

Gawain, Shakti. *Creative Visualization* (Whatever Publishing: California, 1978).

Giles, Herbert A. *Chuang Tzu* (Unwin, 1980).

Herrigel, Eugen. *Zen in the Art of Archery* (Routledge Kegan Paul, and Associated Book Publishers [UK] Ltd, 1953).

Hesse, Herman. *Demian* (Peter Owen, London, 1960).

Hyams, Joe. *Zen in the Martial Arts* (Bantam, 1982).

Jung, Carl G. *Synchronicity* (Routledge Kegan Paul, and Associated Book Publishers [UK] Ltd, 1972).

Lau D.C. *The Analects* (Penguin Classics, 1979).

Legeza, Laszlo. *Tao Magic* (Thames and Hudson, 1975).

Liang, Master T.T. *T'ai Chi Ch'uan* (Vintage, 1977).

Lo, Benjamin Pang Jen. *The Essence of T'ai Chi Ch'uan* (North Atlantic Books: California, 1979).

Maslow, Abraham. *The Farther Reaches of Human Nature* (Penguin Books, 1976).

Merton, Thomas. *The Way of Chuang Tzu* (Unwin, 1970).

Needham, Joseph. *Science and Civilization in China* (Cambridge University Press, 1974).

Ni, Hua Ching. *Tao* (The Shrine of the Eternal Breath of Tao: California, 1979).

Overmyer, Daniel L. *Religions of China* (Harper & Row, 1986).

Ralston, Peter. 'Consciousness and the Martial Arts,' *Human Resource Potential* (Hendon, London).

Rawson and Legeza. *Tao* (Thames and Hudson, 1973).

Rosbach, Sara. *Feng Shui* (Hutchinson, 1984).

Salamah, Siti. 'Systems Methodologies and Isomorphies,' *Proceedings of the Society for General Systems Research* (Intersystems Publications, 1984).

Skinner, Stephen. *The Living Earth Manual of Feng Shui* (Routledge Kegan Paul, and Associated Book Publishers [UK] Ltd, 1979).

Watts, Alan. *Tao, the Watercourse Way* (Penguin Books, 1979).

Wen Kuan Chu. *Tao and Longevity* (Weiser, 1984).

Wen-shan Huang. *Fundamentals of T'ai Chi Ch'uan* (South Sky Book Co: Hong Kong, 1979).

Wilhelm, Richard. *The Secret of the Golden Flower* (Routledge Kegan Paul, and Associated Book Publishers [UK] Ltd, 1965).

Index